Empowering stories of c

Campfire for the Heart
Stories of Resilience

Lindy Chamberlain-Creighton, Matt Golinski,
Gayle Shann, Steve Parish OAM, Yarraka
Bayles, Chad Staples and more ...

BIG SKY PUBLISHING
www.bigskypublishing.com.au

Natalie Stockdale

Big Sky Publishing Pty Ltd
PO Box 303, Newport, NSW 2106, Australia
Phone: 1300 364 611
Fax: (61 2) 9918 2396
Email: info@bigskypublishing.com.au
Web: www.bigskypublishing.com.au

Cover design and typesetting: Think Productions
Printed and bound in Australia by Griffin Press

A catalogue record for this
book is available from the
National Library of Australia

Author: Natalie Stockdale
Title: Campfire for the Heart: Stories of Resilience
ISBN: 978-1-922765-59-8

Empowering stories of overcoming adversity

Campfire for the Heart

Stories of Resilience

Lindy Chamberlain-Creighton, Matt Golinski,
Gayle Shann, Steve Parish OAM, Yarraka
Bayles, Chad Staples and more ...

BIG SKY PUBLISHING
www.bigskypublishing.com.au

Natalie Stockdale

Thank you to everyone who contributed to this book – the generous storytellers who kindly trusted me with their personal journeys, and exemplify that 'It's not what happens to you, but how you react to it that matters.'

I also wish to thank my girls, who would nudge me along with an occasional, 'Come on, hurry up!'

As this book was written from my boat, I'd also like to thank my marina mates, Paul Dawson and Cate MacKenzie, for their support.

'Alone we can do so little;
together we can do so much.'

Helen Keller

Praise for Campfire for the Heart

With *Campfire for the Heart*, Natalie Stockdale has assembled a broad and thought-provoking collection that shares the often-traumatic experiences of a range of remarkable Australians, including her own. Delivered with humanity, intelligence, compassion and empathy, these stories become more than a record. They form a humbling and inspiring pathway towards a way of being that is elementally uplifting, despite – and in many ways because of – being born of suffering.
Mark Muller – Editor-in-Chief, R.M.Williams OUTBACK magazine

It has been my personal experience that through candour and the simple sharing of the truth that we can collectively create hope, and change. So, I absolutely commend Natalie on this beautiful project of stories of such hope.
Shanna Whan – Founder of Sober in the Country, 2022 Australian Local Hero of the Year

Campfire for the Heart, an amazing book by Natalie Stockdale, is a book for all ages. It is inspiring and resilient. I hope this book becomes a runaway success.
Dr Arun Gandhi – Founder/President, M.K. Gandhi Institute for Nonviolence, Rochester, NY

The human brain is wired to recite and hear great stories. Neuroeconomist Paul Zak discovered that when you tell a story, your brain releases a burst of the love hormone, oxytocin. Natalie Stockdale has created the ultimate oxy-bomb within her collection of inspirational stories of resilience and perseverance. With the alarming statistics around male suicide, I'm personally grateful to Natalie for bringing the thoughts, feelings and experiences of 30 men and women, to her symbolic campfire. Thank you, Natalie.

Rae Bonney – Vice President, Australian Men's Health Forum

When we share stories, spoken directly from our heart, they can have a profound effect on those listening. The 'campfire' stories, curated by Natalie Stockdale, expose the raw vulnerability of humans, along with our capacity to conquer our darkest times. Compelling and healing.

Amber Petty – Author of This is Not a Love Song

Campfire for the Heart offers rich, diverse, and sometimes raw stories of resilience, which will inspire and perhaps guide any reader. The stories are so effective because they speak to our shared humanity, each in their own way. We are reminded, again and again, how frail we are as a species, but also how extraordinarily capable we are at surviving, and even thriving, against all odds. While some stories may resonate more with the reader than others, all have elements of grace, humility and strength. May the cup of your heart be filled with these.

Dr Jean Renouf – Founder and Chair, Resilient Byron

Campfire for the Heart provides a gut-wrenching compilation of stories where those who have encountered their worst nightmare are able to not only recount how they survived, but often how they thrived in the face of seemingly unbearable tragedy.

Dr Alexandra Wake – Associate Professor in Journalism, RMIT University

Contents

FOREWORD 1
Dr Craig Challen, Co-Australian of the Year 2019

INTRODUCTION 4

CHAPTER 1: WRAPPED IN LOVE BY AUSTRALIA 9
Matt Golinski: Rising from the death of my wife and
children in a house fire.

CHAPTER 2: THE LION-HEARTED NURSE...........................15
Robyn Hill: Rising from my trauma as a nurse in Sudan and
Rwanda.

CHAPTER 3: WINGS OF HOPE..25
Kwame Selormey: Rising from despair, to who I am today.

CHAPTER 4: FROM KABUL TO THE BLUE MOUNTAINS 35
Esmat Noori: Rising from Taliban terror in Afghanistan and
detention in Indonesia to my immigration to Australia.

CHAPTER 5: HAPPINESS IS A CHOICE 43
Lindy Chamberlain-Creighton: Rising from the loss of
my baby Azaria, public and media vilification, wrongful
imprisonment, and divorce.

CHAPTER 6: WHEN THE PIANO STOPPED PLAYING............51
Alannah McGregor: Rising from the loss of two of my
children through suicide.

CHAPTER 7: QUADEN'S LAW 57

Yarraka Bayles: Dealing with my son's disability, bullying and public vilification.

CHAPTER 8: UNDER A COOLIBAH TREE 65

Hugh (Bill) O'Connor: Rising from an accident that caused the loss of my leg, then continuing to run a vast sheep station for 60 years.

CHAPTER 9: SINK OR SWIM 73

Gayle Shann: Rising from a farm accident that destroyed my arms.

CHAPTER 10: #6BS 81

Brad Millsteed: Rising from depression and creating a movement for men's health.

CHAPTER 11: LET'S TALK 89

Jetha Devapura: Rising from Obsessive Compulsive Disorder.

CHAPTER 12: THE SHOW GOES ON 101

Ann Ballinger: Rising from grief, while managing our outback sheep station.

CHAPTER 13: GETTING THE JOB DONE 111

Brent Mickleberg MP: Rising from PTSD as a returned soldier.

CHAPTER 14: SAILING FOR SOLACE 119

James Prascevic: Rising from PTSD as a returned soldier.

CHAPTER 15: LOST AT SEA 127

Louise Eacott: Rising from the loss of my family at sea on *Great Expectations*.

CHAPTER 16: A NORTHERN TERRITORY LOVE STORY......133
Bill Brayshaw: Rising from the stolen generation, Cyclone Tracy, and the loss of our son.

CHAPTER 17: MY HEALING COCOON...................141
Antonia Kotsiros: Rising from Parkinson's disease.

CHAPTER 18: DON'T JUDGE A BOOK BY ITS COVER.........147
Dianne Moussa: Dealing with blindness, a spinal disease and constant physical pain.

CHAPTER 19: THE GIFTS OF ADVERSITY 155
Steven Farrugia: Rising from sexual abuse and Crohn's disease.

CHAPTER 20: WARRIOR WOMAN 161
Carolyn: Rising from the sexual abuse of my children and witnessing a horse massacre.

CHAPTER 21: BACK IN THE SADDLE...................167
Jamie Ryder: Rising from a broken back and bankruptcy.

CHAPTER 22: A LIFE OF PASSION AND PURPOSE...............175
Steve Parish OAM: How a lifelong passion for inspiring others to connect to nature provided strength when life's challenges seemed insurmountable.

CHAPTER 23: NOT ON MY WATCH 183
Chad Staples: Rising from bushfires that ravaged our zoo.

CHAPTER 24: A VOICE FOR THE VOICELESS 191
Sara Tilling: Rising from the ashes after a catastrophic bushfire.

CHAPTER 25: LIGHT BULB MOMENTS 199
Mark Tregellas: Rising from police-work trauma.

CHAPTER 26: SECOND CHANCE 207
Adam Smith: Rising from depression, attempted suicide and my subsequent disabilities.

CHAPTER 27: THE EPIPHANY THAT SAVED ME FROM SUICIDE 213
Mal Missingham: Rising from depression, alcoholism and the brink of suicide.

CHAPTER 28: THE INSTINCTIVE WARRIOR........................219
Jeff Hansen: Rising from depression to a life of passion and adventure.

CHAPTER 29: THE FLYING NUN 229
Sister Anne Maree Jensen: Rising to my calling as a flying nun.

CHAPTER 30: KEEPING THE SNAKE OUTSIDE....................239
Natalie Stockdale: Rising from droughts, divorce and disease.

AFTERWORD 259
A Tribute to the Human Spirit

ABOUT THE AUTHOR..261

Foreword

Dr Craig Challen, Co-Australian of the Year 2019

C*ampfire for the Heart* is filled with stories of human trials and recovery.

We will all face a great test in our lives. This can come in many forms, and there is no telling when it may arrive. It is a personal thing – that which will be a trial for one person may feel mundane to, or even be barely recognised by, another. Some of the plights are common in history and instantly recognisable to most of us: illness in ourselves or someone close to us, the disappointment of failing to achieve a cherished goal, finding yourself in the midst of war or natural disaster. Others will be unique to the person experiencing them.

The first step in meeting the challenge is understanding that you cannot, by and large, control the circumstances with which you are faced. What you *can* control is how you respond to those circumstances. The choice you make – whether to succumb to the challenge or to rise to it and look adversity in the eye and overcome it – is what defines you as a person.

When I meet people that have faced great challenges, I am often impressed that they regard the adversity they have been through as a gift, an event that may not have been pleasant at the time but has ultimately improved them as a person, making then better and stronger. For these people, the high point of their lives has been the moment that they made that decision to overcome and triumph. From that moment on, it all became much easier defeating the challenge, and passing the test was merely a matter of filling in the details.

Looking at it this way might give the impression of trivialising the experiences.

However, that couldn't be further from the truth.

We have a great deal to learn from observing how others have dealt with their tests. Because of the unpredictable nature of the challenges we face, one might think that we cannot prepare for them. In fact, there is much we can do to make ourselves ready. Broadly, this can be described as increasing resilience. Think of it as your life up to that point being spent in training to equip yourself with the skills, experiences and attitudes that will best prepare you for the task.

To my mind, the most important areas of attention are:

- maintaining your health (both mental and physical) to the highest standards possible

- learning as much as you can about subjects outside your area of expertise, which you might bring to bear when lateral thinking is required

- attempting hard things to give yourself the chance to practise in struggle and accustom yourself to embracing failure as a chance to learn, grow and become stronger

- avoiding the temptation to spend your life evading inconvenience and minor discomfort.

And above all else, take responsibility for your decisions and your destiny. This is the *sine qua non* of a successful life.

The stories to follow also repeatedly talk of the value of gratitude for the gifts that we have and the experiences that are visited upon us. Those are the lessons of the stories in Natalie Stockdale's book.

All of this is succinctly summarised in the words of that great philosopher and observer of human nature: Ricky Gervais: 'You shouldn't try to pave the jungle, you should put on better boots.'

Introduction

According to an Aboriginal proverb:

'We are all visitors to this time, this place.
We are just passing through.
Our purpose here is to observe,
to learn, to grow, to love ...
and then we return home.'

Sometimes, while on 'this place', we feel so enlivened that we want time to stop. Other times are so unbearable that we may want *life* to stop.

Well-known holocaust survivor and author, Viktor Frankl, from Austria, believed that through suffering, we find meaning in life. He said, 'Suffering is an ineradicable part of life, even as fate and death. Without suffering and death, human life cannot be complete.'

I wrote this book to explore how people manage their suffering successfully, and to shed light on the various keys to human resilience. By learning how other people have dealt with their hardships, we can learn from their experiences and be better prepared for our own.

I was once asked by a client, who was suffering with anxiety, 'How do *other* people cope? How do *other* people make the pain go away?'

These questions are answered in the following true stories, generously and often bravely shared by people who have recovered from ordeals – the death of loved ones, major injuries, diseases, bushfires, droughts, war, Taliban terror, displacement, violence, abuse, bankruptcy, bullying and injustice. Although each story is unique, they all showcase the power of resilience and illuminate pathways to happiness for us all.

For community and species survival, humans are hardwired to learn from storytelling. It's through the sharing of stories (traditionally around a campfire) that we pass experience and wisdom through generations.

Each storyteller shared their story by responding to a set of questions, either verbally in an interview, or in writing. Their responses were then loosely woven into a map of life experience known as the 'Hero's Journey'.

According to Joseph Campbell, an American mythological researcher who wrote *The Hero with a Thousand Faces*, humans are programmed to transcend hard times. Campbell noticed that every story and myth – spanning every tribe and culture around the world, regardless of geography and time – shared the same structure.

His 'map' of personal transformation not only 'normalises' hard times, it gives them value. By understanding the Hero's Journey, we're advantaged by knowing that when we rise from our ordeals, we gain more experience, wisdom and strengths – this then empowers us to overcome our next challenges.

Like the four seasons, the Hero's Journey is cyclical. The journey begins at the end of what came before. You depart from your comfort zone, set forth into an adventure, sometimes reluctantly, other times by choice. You experience hardships, engage your resources, recover with new strengths and wisdom, then finally return to a new comfort zone.

The 'campfire' storytellers in this book are the heroes of their journeys.

By learning how other people have converted their darkest times to personal growth and success, you may discover how you too can learn and grow from your hardships, how you can be the hero of your journey.

While we're 'just passing through' this place, let's observe, learn, grow and love together.

Welcome to our campfire.

Introduction

Chapter 1

Wrapped in Love by Australia

Matt Golinski

**Rising from the death of my wife and
children in a house fire.**

*'Life doesn't always follow the script you've written,
and when it takes a different direction, you've
simply got to pick up and head in that direction.'*

Rachael Golinski

I was born to be a chef. I knew that as a young boy. Then in high school, I chose subjects of Art, Home Economics and French to support my culinary ambitions. I completed my apprenticeship in Brisbane and travelled throughout Australia and the world with my wonderful wife, Rachael.

Together we created an idyllic family life on the Queensland coast with our three young daughters – Sage and Willow (twins) and Starlia – and our dog. Rachael was a nurse, and I had a catering business and was a chef on the television program, *Ready Steady Cook*.

My life took a tragic turn in the early hours of Boxing Day in 2011. Our Christmas tree with fairy lights caught fire and engulfed our entire house. Rachel died while trying to protect Sage and Willow. Driven away by the heat, my efforts to save Starlia were also unsuccessful. Two months later, covered in burns to 40 percent of my body, I woke up in hospital from an induced coma. My first instinct was to ask for a phone to call Rachael.

'I'm sorry, mate, they're all gone,' my father told me.

My burn treatments – painful skin grafts and physiotherapy – continued in hospital for another two months. I lost 22 kilograms, could hardly see, and could not talk or eat properly. My elbows calcified and were locked at right angles. My heart, liver, kidneys and lungs were all damaged.

Although the physical pain was intense, it was insignificant compared to the emotional pain of losing my family. Why, I wondered, did they bother keeping me alive? What makes them think I'd want to still be alive?

Traumatic as it was, I'll always remember the hospital staff with gratitude. All the staff, including the cleaners, became my friends. Their support lifted me. In fact, the support

I received from the whole country lifted me. I remember receiving a cheque, for example, for $22.50 from a man in Perth who raised funds for me by selling muffins. I'll always appreciate everyone who showed me that they cared. I felt I was wrapped in love by Australia. I thought that if family, friends and strangers were going to put their love and energy into wanting me to survive, then I was going to work really hard to do it.

On my first night out of hospital, I stayed at my father's place and, although I could barely hold a knife, I managed to cook a stir-fry for a few friends. That was an important milestone in my recovery. I thought that if I could cook again, I'd be ok. Cooking for people has always been and continues to be a passion for me because I get to show off and give to people at the same time.

However, I then spent about four months crying and screaming and asking myself why this tragedy happened. And of course, I did some heavy drinking and all that sort of stupid stuff to numb the pain. Eventually, though, I just accepted that bad things happen and there is absolutely nothing you can do to change it.

Rachael had begun writing a book about our family, and in it, she said that 'life doesn't always follow the script you've written, and when it takes a different direction, you've simply got to pick up and head in that direction'. These words gave me strength to pick myself up. Accepting what you can't control and focusing on what you can control was helpful.

Being creative with music also gave me joy. My mother taught me how to play the guitar when I was eight. I also took up drums and began weekly piano lessons. Music definitely played a role in my recovery.

I also knew that I'd feel better by improving my physical fitness, so I started setting running goals for myself. The first was to complete a five-kilometre fun run, then ten-kilometre runs and eventually half marathons. It wasn't easy with all my injuries, but I was determined. Over time, I gradually increased the distance of my daily runs and peaked with a full marathon and a 96-kilometre Kokoda challenge in the Gold Coast hinterland in 24 hours.

I don't run in gyms or along streets. I leave my phone behind and run in the bush, breathing in the fresh air and scents of the bush as I go. I practise mindfulness as I run, by focusing on everything that's around me – the trees, the flowers, the sounds of the birds and the smell of honey in natural beehives. By running mindfully, I connect to the seasons and am reminded that the world isn't all bad. I always return home feeling better after a run.

My emotional recovery also involved detaching from my grief by parking the tragedy where it belongs – in the past. The sadness still comes sometimes, but I don't hang on to it. If I think about my girls for a while, and the times we had, it becomes too sad and takes me backwards.

Unfortunately, I had to let go of some people in my life because they didn't or couldn't detach themselves from the event. They held on to the grief. I hope those people who I left behind understand this.

For a long time, I was challenged by the milestone days such as birthdays, and by memorable places we shared. I wanted nothing to do with Christmas for five years after the fire and used to fall into a heap when seeing a place by a river where we enjoyed fish and chips. Later, however, I learnt that we have a choice in how to react whenever we're triggered.

We can be depressed by the memories or cherish them. Now, when I see that place by the river, I'm thankful for the great times we had there.

During my rehabilitation process, I met another kind and wonderful woman, Erin Yarwood. Erin was a fitness trainer, and I noticed the sincere compassion she showed to her clients, who were all in vulnerable situations like me.

Following a long friendship, our relationship deepened, and we were engaged in 2016. We have since been blessed with a five-year-old daughter, Aluna, and Tillie Rose, who was born on Christmas Day in 2021. My girls are my little rays of sunshine.

I am blessed now with a rich and fulfilling life with Erin, Aluna, Tillie Rose, and our dogs, Gypsy and Daisy. We have great friends, supportive families, and both love our work. Currently, I'm the Consultant Executive Chef at Peppers Resort in Noosa. I also travel around Australia as a guest chef at festivals and events and write in food columns. I love the Sunshine Coast and the world-class food that is grown here. I could improve my work/life balance, but overall, I feel fit, healthy and happy.

The various ways I've adapted to the tragedy in my life may or may not work for everyone, but my advice to people who are suffering is to appreciate what you have. Appreciate everything around you. This morning, I had toast and a 'babycino' in bed with Aluna. I cherished that time. There's always something to be grateful for. Secondly, find exercise that you enjoy. Move your body. Finally, don't be afraid to ask for help. Most people give generously when they're needed.

Chapter 2

The Lion-Hearted Nurse

Robyn Hill

Rising from my trauma as a nurse in Sudan and Rwanda.

'If I can get through Sudan, I can get through anything.'

I have always seen the world empathetically and made important life choices via a snap decision with no fear, just sheer naïve excitement and goodwill. Some of those decisions have led to extraordinary life experiences and others have been extremely hard lessons.

Growing up in Tamworth, New South Wales, I listened to my father's travel stories and knew without doubt that this would also be my future. Further inspired by *Out of Africa*, I decided to be a nurse in Africa. More than a fanciful whim, it became a single-minded dedication.

My dream was realised in 1996, when I was twenty-six.

I was amazed and disgusted by Africa in equal measure. Fascinated by its wildlife and landscapes, I was also incensed at the imbalance of poverty and wealth. I could not get my head around it and felt I needed to help.

While looking for a job as a nurse, I lived in Nairobi and painted overland trucks. After an evening of tall stories around a campfire, I noticed two pairs of eyes fixed to my every word. They were eavesdropping missionaries who told me they were taking six pallets of donated medical supplies from South Africa to Sudan and asked me if I could help itemise the goods. I agreed and started the next day.

They spoke about Sudan as if it was an untouched paradise. They admitted that the country was at war and had been for over 50 years, but they never saw anything like that. It was a peaceful place and their favourite country, a country too good to miss! Would I join them, they asked – 'It will only be three days!'

Naturally, I said yes!

In Maridi, we went to the hospital where the medical supplies were to be delivered. The hospital was utterly disintegrated. The walls were splattered with bullet holes and fractures. The floor was littered with blood-stained theatre equipment and shells from air attacks.

One day, upon returning to a compound, we were immediately detained by the Sudanese Peoples Liberation Army (SPLA), and the six pallets of medical supplies were stolen from us. We were then taken to another town, Mundri, and held captive in a compound under armed guard. After a long meeting with the missionaries and the governor of the SPLA – which I was not allowed to attend – it was agreed that the missionaries would be allowed to complete their 'mission'.

Until this time, I had known nothing of the true reason behind the journey: to deliver bibles to the frontline of the military activity. The missionaries had bargained off all the medical supplies *and me!* In return, they could keep their bibles and conduct their ministry to the soldiers. The deal was that I would treat the SPLA's wounded soldiers by using 'our' medical supplies. I was the missionaries' bargaining chip!

The average age of these 'soldiers' in the SPLA was about 13 years old. Their uniforms engulfed their bodies, which were dwarfed by their rifles. Although I was the only woman there, I strangely didn't feel threatened by them. When they made lewd gestures towards me, I just ignored them. Whenever I washed myself, I did so with my clothes on and kept my passport in my boot ALWAYS. Food was scarce, so to survive, I stole S26 baby formula (from the medical supplies) and choked down rats and bats caught by the soldiers. As a result, we were all extremely sick.

At night, I would stare at the moon and 'talk' to my mum and dad, 'willing' them to know that I was alive and that I would get home. It was a terrifying experience and one that, at that time, had no end in sight. Whenever I asked when we could leave, they said, 'There'll be a truck for you tomorrow' … but the truck never came.

Thirty-nine days later, one of the missionaries almost died of cerebral malaria. My attempts to treat him were unsuccessful, and we were granted a trip under armed guard back to Maridi to seek urgent help. On our way to Maridi, I saw workers from the United Nations and Medicans Sans Frontier. I figured that this was the best opportunity I may ever have to escape.

So, I jumped out of the moving truck and ran to safety. I was immediately embraced and flown to Nairobi.

Having not quenched my inquisitive nature, nor my naive 'save the world' attitude, I had to 'get back on the horse'. In 1996, I continued to work as a nurse in Rwanda in the repatriation phase after the genocide. This experience too was not without trauma.

One night, I heard a gentle tap, tap on my front door. It was a young woman who needed safety from violence for the night. She slept on my floor. The next night, she returned with another woman, then another. Over time, my house was filled with courageous woman; many had their faces torn to shreds from being beaten. I treated their wounds but couldn't leave bandages on them because their secret safety hub would be exposed. Each night, the women talked and shared their stories.

One woman stopped turning up. She was murdered.

Seeing my devastation, one of the other women said to me, 'My dear Robyn, what you see as death, we see as survival. She has gone on to a better life.' Their unwavering faith in God gave them peace. It was the most profound and humbling time of my life. Sometimes, we all need faith and spirituality, whatever that means to you.

I now have a 25-year nursing career, working mostly in developing countries (Indonesia and Papua New Guinea) and with marginalised populations in rural and remote areas of Australia. As you might expect, there are inherent trauma risks in such areas, and they have certainly impacted my life. The things that bring me close to breaking point are not the horrific injuries to humans or animals. We nurses can learn to prepare for them. What I find most challenging is what humans are capable of doing to each other, and the sheer horror that comes from that. Secondly, it is my *perceived* inability to affect change. My sense of failure settled heavily in my mind and was my biggest downfall.

Going into Sudan, for me, was a pivotal odyssey that became a benchmark for future life experiences. 'If I can get through Sudan, I can get through anything' became my mantra. This attitude, however, was unhealthy and unsustainable. It drove me to extremely difficult work situations. I was setting unachievable goals, and over time, I became highly critical of myself. I adopted the habit of gathering stress and not resilience, then wondered why I felt so miserable.

Finally, I had an epiphany. No achievements could appease my self-esteem while I had low self-worth. I had to stop this self-flagellation habit and start being kind to myself. I was not respecting myself, nor the people who had expressed their concern and love for me. I didn't have to make gargantuan, world-saving changes. It is the little things that matter. Small, achievable goals, such as making a difference in one person's life each day.

When I decided to be kind to myself, I made healthy adjustments to my life. For example, I removed myself from people who did not have my best interests at heart, who used my vulnerabilities against me. Some people see giving yourself a hard time as permission for them to do the same, and they do it with relentless obsession. It was liberating to recognise this and free myself from them. I have been blessed with a loving, large, extended family, as well as an extraordinary community of friends who remind me of my worth. I now choose to surround myself only with positive, supportive people.

I have also been blessed with other people who have entered my soul deeply. People who I will never forget. Impoverished people who offered me kindness and care, and their innermost truth. Victims of unspeakable crimes, conflict and illness, who have continuously tried to balance joy with their tragedy. I am blessed to have been a witness of their courage and, in their memory, I give them my gratitude. Life is so tough sometimes, and it's hard to turn grief and fear into strength and courage. I am inspired by the people who go beyond their oppressions and inequalities, pull themselves together and carry on.

I maintain my 'if I can get through Sudan, I can get through anything' mantra, but I have let go of the high expectations. I dug deeply into what peace and resilience means to me now and realise that there is no 'one size fits all' solution. Sometimes our coping strategies lose their potency and effect. We need an arsenal of strategies so that if one strategy fails, we can try a new one.

Gratitude is a powerful strategy. My beloved mother recently died – it was an event I feared all my life. I am grateful for the life our family had with her. I am grateful that she is no longer in pain. I did absolutely everything that was humanly possible to ensure Mum had some quality of life in her final years ... and I am at peace with that.

Acts of kindness also help. When I am sad, I volunteer to help someone local. It gives me a sense of worth and joy. I cook. My friends and I have a casual community cooking arrangement. I cook up a big batch of something and share it with friends who live on their own or who are struggling. My friends then do the same the following week. We choose to eat alone or share company. I have a fire-pit and often say, 'You are welcome at my campfire anytime.'

Be realistic and accept that pain is a part of life's experiences.

We can choose to stay there and feed it, or break away from it. Accept that there are highs and lows in life. It would be foolish to think that once we get over something it is 'up, up and away'. With resilience, we manage the lows, so they don't stay and are not as severe.

Integrity is a magnificent quality for resilience. If someone treats you badly and you have done what you thought was right, walk away with your head held high. If someone chooses to walk away from you, let them. Don't beg for anyone to treat you with respect, and don't be frightened to say no or state what you want. It's YOUR relationship too.

Be aware of your thoughts and words. Thoughts and words have energy. Instead of the word 'suffering', which portrays powerlessness and failure, I say 'living with', which portrays survival and strength. I dropped the word 'should' from my vocabulary. I no longer say, 'I should be this' or 'I should be doing that'. That's just negative!

You create reality with your own thoughts. Darkness cannot survive in the presence of the smallest amount of light. Light illuminates darkness. Through your thoughts, let in the light, even just a bit. Humorous thoughts and words often help. It's ok to laugh, even in times of grief. Good friends can sledge each other. I even sledge myself – kindly.

Writing this has been both difficult and cathartic. Some of these experiences have left deep scars that I hold so privately and dearly, but I am ever grateful to be alive and to write anything at all. I recount these events in humble hope that at best they may be useful prompts for reflection. At worst, they may provide entertaining solace for people struggling with the same issues.

Be kind to yourself. Be kind to others.

Chapter 2

Photo by Therese Ritchie

Chapter 3
Wings of Hope

Kwame Selormey

Rising from despair, to who I am today.

'I am not what happened to me,
I am what I choose to become.'

Carl Jung

My name Kwame means 'Saturday'. I arrived on Earth on a Saturday, and the Earth named me while my parents had about seven days to get to know my soul a bit better before giving me the name I deserved. My last name, Selormey, (traditionally - eSe-Lo-Ame) means 'lovers of life and souls'.

My country, where my spirit belongs, is the volta region of Ghana. We are the Ewe (pronounced Eveh) people – a small minority tribe who live by the ocean and have a history dating back to the 11th century.

My mother hails from the Togolese Republic, and while we grew up in Ghana, my brothers and I often crossed the national borders to Togo to pay homage to our other ancestral lands and spend time with our cousins.

My mother was a teacher and, through sheer determination, broke the mould of poverty that she grew up in. My father was a mechanical engineer and excelled at it for many years. He was a quiet and humble man, who chose his company carefully.

Even though I had a nuclear family of my parents and brothers, there were many other people who played a significant role in caring for my brothers and me, particularly my maternal grandmother and aunt. Both women often lived with us.

My grandmother was called Mama Xose, which translated into 'the old lady of faith'. She was a blind woman with grey eyes, very few teeth, and she was always traditionally dressed. She had a soothing voice and had a story for every event that occurred in life. When things were dark, she told stories of light. When things were bright, she told stories of the darkness. One could say she was committed to ensuring we always remembered balance.

Her own life had been fraught with misfortune, especially as a woman with a disability and who had lost many children to stillbirths before my mother and her siblings came along.

My aunty, Atsufui Rose, was born with her twin brother. She had cerebral palsy, and at an early age, lost her hearing and later contracted polio, which lead her to becoming further disabled. She was deaf and mute. However, she made particular sounds my brothers and I learnt to understand over time. We called her 'Tailor', because she taught herself to sew clothes and went on to becoming a tailor. Because of the adversity that she went through to learn the skills she had, she beamed every time she watched our lips say Tailor, and that was how she carried her worth as a woman who contributed.

Growing up, I was intrigued by observing things around me. The greatest teacher I had was not in a classroom. It was in the things I saw outside in the streets, the booming laughter from passers-by, the wailing cries amid ululations of grief at funerals, the side stories overheard in market squares, and the unforgettable smells that linked everything together.

Mama Xose and Tailor often travelled together. One of them provided the eyes, and the other provided the physical strength. One of my earliest recollections from observing them is the moment of realisation that we can never do everything alone in this world.

Growing up in the 70s and 80s was on an incredible bitter-sweet backdrop of some remarkable events.

The bitterness was characterised by at least seven military coup d'états, featuring heinous assassinations by firing squads, which occurred in succession to each military takeover of Ghana; sudden curfews causing us all to scurry home for shelter and safety; mass deportations of Ghanaians who were living in Nigeria under the Shehu Shagari regime; arriving in Ghana by truckloads like cattle piled on top of each other and localised armed robberies due to social poverty.

The sweet part was the bubble of safety that my parents had created for my siblings and me in the early days, and the various innovative approaches they took to ensure that we had food on the table. We experienced many adventures in the name of survival, which ranged from selling fish, charcoal and cool drinks, to chickens, cattle and pigs. One of my favourite innovative missions was when my father invented and built an oven for baking bread. The waft of fresh bread filling the air every morning is a treasured memory.

Occasionally, my father took us out hunting for grasscutters (large rat-like animals) followed by rituals of blessing the animal for its sacrifice and giving gratitude to it for the life it helped preserve.

In the meantime, my grandmother consistently counteracted every bitter moment with a sweet story that gave hope even when hope itself was afraid. She'd also tell us about the rarest treasure in the world hidden somewhere safe, and how our mission was to look everywhere for that treasure. However, if it was ever found, it had to be given away quickly, or humanity would perish. I later came to realise that the treasure she often referred to was 'kindness'. It helped to know that others were searching for it too, and that one day, I would be on the receiving end of it and give it away.

When I was around 12, an event occurred that changed our lives, and if hope and resilience was a person, my whole family would have been calling out to him/her to hear us, save us and guide us.

My four brothers and I were sleeping in our bedroom, and my parents and my youngest brother were in their room. We heard a truck pull up outside the gates of our house. As we peered down from the second storey of the tiny house, we saw armed men dressed in black climbing out of the truck and surrounding the house with guns in their hands. My brother whispered to us that they were armed robbers, and this was bad.

They climbed over the fence in vast numbers like black rats filling the compound. My mother ran into our room with my little brother and told us all to stay under the bed. Then shooting began. There was only a couple of shots. My mother asked us all to cover our ears. This was followed by a loud shot, which was close to us.

She asked us to stay quiet. We froze. Not one of us cried. She crawled back to the other room to check on my dad. Then, after what felt like a long time, we all crept to the window and looked down. The men were climbing out of the compound, just like they climbed in, then got into the truck and drove off.

Our parents returned to our room, soothed us and told us to go back to bed. Everything was quiet … until we heard heavy footsteps outside. One more man was trying to climb over the wall. He fell to the ground and didn't move. As light came, it became evident that he had died.

By daylight, our house was surrounded by crowds of people, including the police. The body was removed, and my father was exonerated due to the circumstances under which he took that shot. However, a life had been lost that day, whether intentional or not. We who bear the name that reminds us to love and protect lives, had taken a life. We had inadvertently crossed a cultural and ethical boundary.

So that night, as the blood was being scrubbed from the concrete floors, my father's self-respect and that of our family was being erased, together with any shred of dignity. The sweet had now separated from the bitter, leaving the bitter to seep through all that was left of us.

During my teenage years, I heard the story of the Sankofa in fragments. A story about a mythical bird that flew through time with its head turned backwards while it carried an egg in its mouth. Some said that it had its head turned backwards to remember its past and cherish it. Some said it was protecting its future – the egg – from the head winds. And some said it was learning the lessons of its past to grow a new future.

Day by day, I continued to absorb everything I was seeing and hearing. I then eventually realised that we are all as broken as we are remarkable, and as time went on, I drew more strength from the stories of hope. Hope says, 'All will be ok.' I enjoyed those stories far greater than the stories that said, 'Be careful out there.'

Hope says trust. Caution says mistrust. I soon realised that hope trumps caution.

As the years went by, my parents lost their way with so much grief that hope was sometimes beyond their reach. But they did a good job in teaching six boys the power of hope. This job was reinforced by a blind grandmother and a broken aunty whose main talent was to stitch.

At the age of 16, my father gave me an old, worn-out t-shirt that had a kangaroo on it with a bow around its neck. I walked into my grandmother's room, and she asked me to describe what I was wearing. I described the shirt, and she asked me what kind of animal would have legs like that. I replied, 'I don't know.' She then said that there was not much here anymore for me, and that our light was going to run out if my brothers and I didn't do anything about it. There was a lot of places out there and a lot of kindness.

And so began my journey to reach out into another part of the world.

My brothers and I knew that it wouldn't be easy, but we had enough resilience in us to survive the elements of any world, given the reality of the one we were living in.

Aged 19, I had my last meal with my parents, brothers, Mama Xose, Tailor and all the people of my kin. My father gave me his savings. A ritual was performed, and I took flight like the Sankofa. My head turned to look back, tears streaking down my cheeks as I flew across the lands and seas until I landed on the ground where that strange animal was.

I started again, and one by one, my brothers also made their way out.

Resettling was so painful and confusing. There were streets full of strangers. And I couldn't clearly express my thoughts because I had no words for them anymore. I felt rejected, trapped, alone, hungry, and guilty for leaving my family and kinship behind to perish. Yet, at the same time, I knew hope was with me and them.

Three decades later, I am still growing, healing and learning. I have a very kind partner who continues to teach me about courage, love, vulnerability and determination. I have a remarkable, loving and intelligent adult son and daughter who remind me that peace doesn't have to come at the price of turmoil. I am also blessed to have the first friend I made in Australia, my ex-wife and mother of my children, who continues to teach me about strength and individuality. I am more at peace today because my brothers are safe and settled around the world. My father has sadly passed away, but my mother still leaves in Ghana with my younger brother, who is now also well established.

Professionally, I have made quite a journey. I discovered that all the adversity and broken pieces of my past gave me a gift of compassion to understand people, wherever they are in their life. I pursued studies and a career working for humanity, rather than for money.

Today I am the CEO of a humanitarian, not-for-profit organisation in the Northern Territory that supports the resettlement of people who were once refugees and migrants into Australia and supports survivors of torture and trauma. I also contribute to various boards that support Australia's humanitarian programs. I have recently had the honour of being a NT Australian of the Year finalist for 2022.

Many things have helped me to heal and recover from challenging times – having supportive people in my life, my staunch sense of hope and optimism that darkness always turns into light, service to humanity, practising kindness, being creative (through dancing, writing and photography) and not losing sight of the stories that have carved me. I do not let these stories, however, hold me back from unravelling the mystery of what I am becoming or yet to become. I am still growing. This is not a journey with a finite recovery end determined by time. It is, however, a process of self-acceptance, re-framing, knowing the impact I have on others and taking pride in the scars that adorn me beautifully.

Every day, everywhere, humanity is suffering. We are all vulnerable, breakable, and capable of recovering.

The words of Carl Jung ring true: 'I am not what happened to me, I am what I choose to become.' The past teaches us about what happened. The lessons are always there, but the classroom changes. I truly believe that suffering is necessary and bears gifts of wisdom, resilience and hope.

Chapter 4

From Kabul to the Blue Mountains

Esmat Noori

Rising from Taliban terror in Afghanistan and detention in Indonesia to my immigration to Australia.

'My dream was to become a lawyer and help women's rights in Afghanistan.'

B eing born in 1989, my childhood in Afghanistan was tough. Hiding from bombs and bullets was the norm. When the Taliban arrived, life became tougher. Women were forced to stay home unless accompanied by a man. Beating people, shooting women, and cutting off hands on the street were common under the lawless, terror-driven Taliban regime. Afghanistan was being destroyed educationally, culturally and historically.

The Taliban hosted a football game one day to entice a big crowd. In the middle of the game, they dragged a woman onto the oval and shot her in front of the crowd. Her crime – being in a relationship with a man without a marriage certificate.

My dream was to become a lawyer and help women's rights in Afghanistan. To that end, I studied law at university in Kabul each day and worked as a bartender for international patrons in the British Embassy each night, supporting my mother and sister. Deprived of all their freedoms, women in Afghanistan need a man to support them.

The selling and consuming of alcohol was outlawed by the Taliban, and they killed people for non-compliance. My job at the embassy was therefore covert. Somehow, however, the Taliban discovered my job and entered our house while I was at work. Mercilessly, they beat my mother, telling her they'd be back to kill me. They left her with lifelong injuries and disabled her – she could never walk again.

I didn't return to my home after that night; I couldn't.

So, I reluctantly fled to Pakistan to replan my life. As much as I wanted to return home and help my mother and sister, it wasn't an option. My mother pleaded with me to stay away. Shocked, confused and depressed, my only way to survive was to escape Pakistan by illegal means.

I was smuggled by plane to Indonesia. In the middle of Jakarta, I was dumped by the smugglers on a busy highway. I had no phone, no contacts, no plan and only $200 in my pocket. Eventually, I found someone who could speak a little English and found my way to the United Nations Office for Refugees. Once approved as a refugee, I had to wait in Indonesian detention centres until a country would accept me.

Those four years were the toughest of my life. For the first two months, I was locked in a hot, putrid cell of two square metres. It had no mattress, fan, or any bedding, with only a toilet, and a bucket and ladle for washing. I shared that cell with nine other men. We slept upon each other in piles. Deprived of fresh air, sunshine, and often fresh water, we became sick, especially with skin diseases. Every day, we would ask ourselves, what did we do wrong? What did we do to deserve this? The worst criminals are treated better than this.

After two months, the cell door opened, and we were allowed to walk around in a yard. I later moved to a slightly better detention centre and started to help a few people speak English. My small, casual group transformed to classes of up to 70 people. The hour-long classes in an airconditioned room gave people a welcome break from the relentless heat.

I tried my best to improve conditions for my fellow refugees. I wrote more than 60 letters to government and non-government organisations, but without any success. Watching the women and children suffer was particularly hard. I always felt helpless.

One day, following an argument with a detention officer who refused to give us water, I became overwhelmed. I wanted to close my eyes and shut down. I went to the bathroom and filled myself with sleeping pills, shampoo, and dishwashing liquid.

Hours later, I woke in hospital, my whole body racked with pain. Psychologists and counsellors asked me why I poisoned myself. 'Nobody is taking action to help these people,' I explained.

Lots of children and families came to visit me in hospital and asked me why I did it. They said, 'We want you to be with us, not here in hospital.'

I'll never forget one eight-year-old girl. She never played with the other kids and was always alone and exposed to things that no child should ever see. She sat on my lap crying and said, 'When do we get out of this place?'

'God is kind,' I told her. 'We'll get out one day.'

That was a turning point. My view of the world expanded. I decided to live, not for myself, but for other people. The nurses asked why so many visitors loved me and came to see me. I told them it was because I loved them. I then apologised to everyone, returned to detention … and everything changed.

The English classes became popular. I even found other English speakers to teach more classes. And I thought there must be other skills among the refugees. Shortly afterwards, painting and craft classes emerged. Volleyball and football games were also played. One day, the chief of immigration thanked me for coming to the detention centre. And I thanked him for not stopping the classes or games. They were important for our wellbeing.

After waiting in Indonesia for four years, Australia thankfully opened its gate to me. I'm now a permanent resident and live in a safe and welcoming community in the Blue Mountains, New South Wales. I work six days a week in Sydney doing construction work while I figure out what to do next.

My dream to help women and children is still alive, but since the fall of Kabul in 2021, the landscape has changed, and I no longer know what my service will look like. The news of Taliban control was distressing. Afghanistan was in chaos with people panicking and dying as they tried to escape. My mother, cousins and friends were in the belly of it.

I felt frustrated that I couldn't help.

The women continue to live in a particularly dangerous situation. When they try to protest, the Taliban beat them or answer with gunfire. Poverty and the collapse of health and education systems are other challenges now facing Afghanistan.

I constantly worry about all the people who just want freedom and happiness like everyone else around the world. Despite the Taliban claiming there is status quo, we know from experience that they cannot be trusted.

Around the same time as the fall of Kabul, I had a COVID vaccine and was hospitalised in extreme pain. As I slowly recovered, I accepted that while I couldn't save 'everyone', I could do my best to help my family evacuate to Pakistan. I filled in hundreds of forms, but the borders closed, and they were trapped.

Although all news from Afghanistan was bleak, I finally found sunlight. My mother received her visa and has just arrived in Australia. After nine years apart, we are now living together. It's so amazing.

I continue to do all I can to help my cousins in Afghanistan, and I think about the many things that make me happy – the support and generosity of Australian communities, the Blue Mountains refugees support group, my new Australian friends, my counsellor, gardens, fresh air, nature and, best of all, having my mum with me in this safe place.

After living without any rights under a terror-led regime, and then in a heinous detention centre when my only 'crime' was escaping from murder, I find it helpful putting hardships into perspective and being grateful for everything that is going well.

In Australia, we have so much to be thankful for – freedom of speech, freedom to work and freedom to be educated. We have legal rights to protect us.

A lot of people constantly want more things, more money, better cars etc. Instead of constantly looking up to get more, we need to look down to *give* more, down to where people need help. Through helping others, we connect and nourish our soul. Through helping others, we find love, purpose and joy.

When I sometimes feel sad, I remember what the children said about loving me, which gives me comfort, for we are nothing without each other. Rather than tormenting myself for not helping thousands of women, I've adapted to the current reality of being able to help one – my mother.

Never give up. You too are wanted and needed.

Chapter 4

Chapter 5
Happiness is a Choice

Lindy Chamberlain-Creighton

Rising from the loss of my baby Azaria, public and media vilification, wrongful imprisonment, and divorce.

'Get out of the shadows and into the sunshine as quickly as you can.'

Background

In August 1980, Lindy Chamberlain's nine-week-old baby Azaria disappeared from their tent at Uluru, Australia, triggering an unprecedented torrent of trauma for Lindy and her family. Thrust into the public spotlight, Lindy not only lost her baby, but she was vilified by the media and public, wrongfully convicted and sentenced to life imprisonment for murdering Azaria and, just weeks after being jailed, she was forced to give up baby Kahlia, who was born while in custody.

Following the discovery of critical evidence that supported her innocence, Lindy was released in 1986, after serving nearly three years in prison. However, it took 32 years after the tragedy before an inquest finally agreed with Lindy's constant claim that baby Azaria was taken by a dingo.

Having suffered layers of grief, injustice, deprivations and prejudice, few people in Australia's modern history are known and admired more for their resilience than Lindy Chamberlain-Creighton.

Before we lost Azaria, we had just moved to Mount Isa in western Queensland. Like any normal family, we were all settling into the new environment and routines. My son Aidan was at his new school. We were getting to know our new local church. Everything was going well.

We decided that a camping trip to Ayers Rock (as it was called then) would be a great adventure for the family and provide excellent photography opportunities. However, one fateful night, Azaria was taken by a dingo at the rock and killed. There were many other terrible things that happened following that, but the hardest was going through my divorce with Michael in 1991.

I believe in the Ten Commandments and God's law, and I therefore take the institution of marriage very seriously. I made a lifetime commitment to Michael and gave my whole heart to make it work, but there were things said and done behind the scenes that made it impossible for us to stay together. I had no desire to leave the marriage, but I had to make a decision that was in the best interest of everyone. It was very hard.

In the Northern Territory in 1982, when I was wrongfully found guilty of murdering Azaria and sentenced to life in prison, a life sentence for white people meant imprisonment until you die, or at the governor's pleasure. It was difficult not knowing my future, but all the way through, I felt positive that God would make sure that I would be exonerated.

I recently learnt about the 'Stockdale Paradox', which was named after someone who was imprisoned in Vietnam during the war. It describes a mindset of unyielding faith that you will prevail, but at the same time, you face the harshness of the situation presented at the time. That's exactly how I coped in prison. I faced what I had to on the spot, as best I could, and I looked forward to the future, knowing that God would never let evil put me through something that He and I couldn't handle together.

Of course, that is different for every person. Evil knows your Achilles heel, but God won't let evil give you anything that you can't handle with his help. God loves you and is always with you, even though you sometimes feel like you are alone.

If I didn't rely on God when I was in prison and let him help me through it, I wouldn't have been able to cope and be there for my remaining children. I had to be there for my children. While I had many letters of support, I was in prison on my own. There was no one inside to support me, but God was with me. God and I knew the truth about Azaria and that was enough for me.

The big gift that came from my experiences was a greater understanding of God and his love. The hard times also gave me additional patience, understanding and knowledge of people. I often help other people who ask how to deal with problems, or how to forgive people who have done them wrong.

I tell them to forgive for their own sake. Leave the chastisement or punishment to God. It's not our job. When you choose to enjoy life, you can't carry anger or resentment. By forgiving, you are giving yourself permission to move on. What happened is not ok, but when you forgive, you're not carrying it. You're giving yourself freedom. What 'they' do, is not what you become. It's on *them*, not on *you*. When people are nasty, it doesn't mean that you have to turn into a nasty person too. You don't have to retaliate with the same venom. You can choose to be nasty or choose not to be.

I let people's nastiness slide off me, and I go forward. The problem is then over. When you do this, you can get on with your life. Perhaps that's the greatest gift that prison gave me.

Forgiveness does not say that you were not hurt. Forgiveness is saying to yourself, I will move forward in my life without regret, anger, and pre-occupation with this. I choose to control my own headspace and be happy. You can let your mind be occupied by regrets, vengeance, or anger, or you can move on. I don't use rear-view mirrors in life.

Pain may be a part of your history, but it doesn't have to be part of your future or your present. Hardships are a part of the foundation of who you are, but they don't have to be all you are. You don't forget, but your ability to deal with things gets better, and time helps too.

Just as God and forgiveness helped me along my journey, so have persistence and determination. Inheriting my Scottish persistence from my father and grandfather, I was determined to have my name cleared not only for my sake, but for my family's sake and future generations.

Courage was also important, courage to face the awful things that happened. When I was in prison, they initially gave me terrible jobs like scrubbing faeces, vomit and snot off walls and floors without gloves. One time, the only tool I was given to clean it all was a toothbrush! Another day, I helped an officer carry a urine-soaked mattress to the dumpster. The urine was dripping onto our feet, sandals and arms, and we were both dry-reaching, but someone had to do it!

Summon your courage to face your fears and just do it. Get it over and done with.

Eleanor Roosevelt said, 'You gain strength, courage, and confidence by every experience in which you really stop to look fear in the face.' You can say to yourself, 'I lived through this horror. I can take the next thing that comes along.' That's exactly what I did. You can choose to like the things you have to do. If you must do something you don't like, ask yourself how you can make it better. I used to have a competition with myself about how fast I could get a job done. Soon, I could do anything asked of me.

Get out of the shadows and into the sunshine as quickly as you can. Deal with the problem, then move on. You don't have to stay in darkness. If you stay there, you get deeper and deeper into the dark shadows. Happiness is a choice. If I feel a bit blue, I pull myself up and make a different choice. Then I realise that life is good again. It doesn't mean that you get what you want all the time, but you don't make yourself miserable if you don't get what you want.

Happiness comes from the inside. It's not something you are owed, and you don't find it outside of you. It's a decision you make. You learn to see good in everything and enjoy what's around you. The glass is half-full. You can choose if you're going to live with anger, regret, revenge, and think yourself a victim, or you can choose to be the hero in your own life, forgive the past and move on. It's true that it's not what happens that counts, it's how you choose to deal with what happens.

Looking back, I can see that my truthfulness also helped me cope with everything. When you're honest and true to yourself, you can look yourself in the mirror and know who you are, unashamed. Truth and justice are always important, so always stand up for the truth.

What is it like being Lindy Chamberlain today?

I've chosen to be happy. I found love again with my second husband, Rick Creighton – God's bonus gift to me! My kids all live on the other side of Australia, but I enjoy Facetime with them and visiting them when it's possible. We're involved in our church community, of course, and I enjoy my crafts, such as making Christmas ornaments. I do some work filing for the National Library archives, and I love designing house plans and interior designs for our home renovation business.

People regularly stop me on the streets and tell me what they've gone through, or they apologise, or are excited to see me because they feel they know me. Some people tell me how my journey has helped them. People didn't hug others outside their family much when I was young, but these days, strangers hug me like I'm a personal friend! Initially it was a shock, but I'm relaxed about it now because I know it comes from good. In fact, it's lovely to think that people feel this way. Sometimes I'm in a hurry and can't stop, but I try to never be rude to people.

My final piece of advice for people who are going through a hard time is for them to get to know God personally. Every burden you have is a shared burden. Handle it together. You are always a winner with God on your side. He is your best friend. Let go of the known for the unknown, and trust God to do what is best for you. Most importantly, get out there and enjoy yourself.

Chapter 6

When the Piano Stopped Playing

Alannah McGregor

Rising from the loss of two of my children through suicide.

'I hold no blame, nor do I have a vendetta.
My only wish is for people to learn from this.'

W̲e had three children. Stuart began work as an apprentice chef aged 17. Stacey was 14 and Angela was 12. Angela and Stuart were very much alike. They were both popular and loved sport and music. Stuart played the piano with passion and sensitivity. They both shared a strong sense of justice and had a wicked sense of humour. My husband worked full-time and I worked part-time on night shifts as a nurse.

Life was good, until … Stuart was physically, verbally and sexually bullied in his workplace. At first, he tried to ignore it, then he tried to tough it out, but eventually it wore him down. The bullying was reported, and he was placed on Workcover.

No longer the easy-going, happy young man with a quick wit, he stopped playing the piano. Instead, he would lie on his bed in a foetal position or rage with anger at the unfairness of it all.

The downward spiral that swiftly followed into the black pit of depression was frightening, confusing and confronting. Diagnosed with anxiety, depression, and post-traumatic stress disorder (PTSD), he was prescribed a cocktail of medications.

About the same time, Stuart began taking cannabis to mask his feelings. He also isolated himself and started self-harming. His downward spiral continued, with suicide attempts and treatments in psychiatric clinics.

Meanwhile, he attended mediations with the bully and ex-colleagues from the human resources department, each time coming away a little more damaged than the time before.

Eventually, the bullying was substantiated, and the perpetrator was offered a package to leave the workplace – instead of being penalised. The injustice devastated Stuart. In his mind, the bully was rewarded.

Workcover then began an investigation with a view of prosecuting the workplace.

Meanwhile, and unbeknown to us, Stuart had been confiding in Angela the extent of the bullying. Being fiercely loyal, Angela became his self-appointed confidant and protector.

We were a family in crisis, barely functioning, and definitely not coping.

Stuart oscillated between darkness in his black pit and lightness in a new life that he was forging. He found a job and enjoyed interacting with his new workmates. He began a relationship with a young woman, and the birth of their beautiful daughter infused us all with hope.

In 2002, three and a half years after Stuart reported the bullying, Workcover completed their investigation and were considering taking the matter to court – an action that resurfaced the trauma for Stuart.

Stuart therefore subsequently spiralled downward into his darkness. And again, we were all drawn into the nightmare cycle of fear and constant vigilance.

Three weeks later, the strain became unbearable for Angela. She came home from school and took her life. Stuart blamed himself. One month later, he too ended his life.

After Angela and Stuart died, I went through all the devastating aspects of grief – denial, disbelief, pain, yearning, loss, tears, guilt, questions and fears – and I finally learnt to live with my grief.

Some things made my journey easier:

- My friends and family who were willing to listen, repeatedly, as I processed and made sense of what happened.

- Knowing that my husband, remaining daughter and granddaughter still needed me.

- The many years of counselling and grief workshops.

- The determination that I would not be another victim and that one day I would be ok.

- Knowing that despite their death, Stuart and Angela remained a part of my life.

- The quotes that gave me the power to get through the tough moments. For example: 'This too shall pass'; 'Just breathe'; 'Accept the things you cannot change'.

- Giving myself time limits to feel pain and grief, then pushing the thoughts out of my head until later.

- Diary and poem writing.

- Self-forgiveness.

- Volunteer work.

- A nutritious diet and vitamin supplements.

- Exercise, despite not wanting to get out of bed.

However, I need to be honest and tell you that there were things that made my grief journey more difficult. The worst of these were judgement and blame. All the questions and guilt associated with suicide deaths had me believe that I had not been a good mother, had not done enough to help, had done too much, had not taught them resilience, had not cared enough, and had not loved them enough.

Eventually, I learnt to accept and forgive myself for my failures, both real and imagined. I learnt that I had done the best that I could with the abilities and knowledge I had at the time.

I believe a person with a 'lived experience' can utilise that experience to instigate changes in the community in a way that no professional can.

I hold no blame, nor do I have a vendetta. My only wish is for people to learn from this. I often talk with families after the death of their loved one by suicide. I feel blessed to be able to do this and hope it helps them find a way through their heartbreak and confusion.

I co-founded the Central Victorian Suicide Prevention Awareness Network to help remove the stigma and break the taboo of suicide. In a safe, stigma-free environment, the Network brings together people bereaved by suicide, so they can openly talk about their deceased loved ones. I continue to volunteer my time in the pursuit of suicide awareness and prevention.

In 2022, I was awarded the inaugural Fred Hollows Humanitarian of the Year Award – the 'Fred Award'. On Australia Day in 2022, I was honoured again with the Bendigo Citizen of the Year Award. I genuinely feel honoured and grateful for the awards and hope that they shine a light on our mission to raise awareness of suicide prevention and the impact of suicide on families and communities.

Life is not so hard these days, though there are still times when the pain returns. I am now able to acknowledge that pain and accept that even though I will always miss Angela and Stuart, I know they are always with me in my thoughts and in my heart.

Yarraka and Quaden Bayles

Chapter 7
Quaden's Law

Yarraka Bayles

**Dealing with my son's disability,
bullying and public vilification.**

'Pain is our biggest teacher.'

Like any other healthy mother in her late twenties, I was thrilled to be expecting another baby – a first son for my partner and I, and a young brother for my twin daughters. As a Murri woman, I come from a big, beautiful family with strong Aboriginal family values and cultural integrity. My partner and I were both working and felt safe and secure.

Quaden's birth was uncomplicated, and we were euphoric about his arrival. Three days later, everything changed. Quaden was diagnosed with achondroplasia, a form of dwarfism, which meant his bones would never grow to their full length. He would require ongoing surgeries and a respiratory machine to help him breathe when sleeping.

I oscillated between denial and depression for about two years. Afterall, my little boy was perfect to me, and still is! My relationship with Quaden's father eventually split under the strain, and I became a single mother.

When Quaden was five, his grandfather (my father) passed away. It was hard for all of us, but particularly for Quaden, as they were very close. Two years later, Quaden's baby brother tragically died at birth. He had been excited about being a big brother. Instead came more grief. Several other deaths in our family occurred around the same time, compounding our grief further.

Protecting, providing and being strong for my children, while in a deep state of grief, was and continues to be a struggle, yet they need me, so I continue.

Caring for Quaden is not for the faint-hearted. Trying to console your crying baby while they are in excruciating pain, begging to die from the pain that comes with his condition, as well as the mental anguish and psychological effects of being born different, accumulatively take a toll.

Quaden was six when I first found him with a rope around his neck to kill himself. This was the first of many more attempts with belts, handbag straps, phone cords, iron cords, towels etc.

I couldn't take my eyes off him, and whenever he was 'too quiet', I prayed against my worst nightmare of finding his lifeless body. This has caused me to live in a state of constant alert and vigilance.

In 2020, when Quaden was 9, the regular bullying at school became untenable. He finally told me he couldn't handle it anymore. Around this time, the Brisbane Bullets basketball team visited his school to play with his class. It was an opportunity too good to miss for a young, sport-loving boy. Quaden was excited and wore his favourite basketball shoes that day.

When I arrived at the school ten minutes early to pick him up, I saw Quaden and his class on the basketball court with the Brisbane Bullets, lining up to get their new singlets signed.

This was when I noticed a group of girls standing around Quaden. One was patting him on the head. They were measuring how tall he was compared to them, while laughing at how small he was.

I wanted to jump in and save my son, but he signalled for me not to. As hard as it was, I respected his decision and watched the bullying from the sidelines. Quaden continued to 'shrug it off', a frequently practised behaviour in the face of unwanted attention that comes from being born different.

As soon as Quaden got his singlet and shoes signed, he stormed to the car and exploded in hysterics.

Despite my best efforts to soothe him, he was inconsolable and wanted to die. In desperation, I told him I would record him live on Facebook so that people could see, hear and feel the impact of their behaviour.

I then asked Quaden what would make him feel better. A pierced ear was the response. So off we went to get his ear pierced. I loved seeing the smile return on his face. He loved his new cool look and was quite impressed with his new 'bling'.

The day finished at home like any other, only to begin again like no other.

The next morning, we were woken early by knocks at the door from media wanting interviews. My phone was ringing non-stop, and messages of love and support were pouring in from all over the world. Our Facebook video had gone viral.

An American comedian with the same condition as Quaden reached out to offer a crowd-funding page to bring Quaden and me to Disneyland for a holiday. Being an independent, single woman, I wasn't particularly comfortable about asking for something, but I didn't think much about it and agreed.

The page reached the $10,000 target in 24 hours and kept going. That's when things took a dark turn.

It seemed the more money that was raised, the more conspiracy theories started to circulate. Then the death threats and hate mail began flooding in from all over the world ... and continues to this day. It impacts our whole family, as we're all targeted.

Strangers would enter through the locked security gates of our gated community, knock on our door and congregate on our private property. Eventually, we packed our bags and sought refuge with other family members, but there was no escaping the madness. It was ubiquitous, yet surreal.

The only thing that got us through emotionally was the unconditional love and support of our family and community.

On the other side of the storm, we are a much stronger and unified family.

We also took practical action to protect ourselves. We enlisted an entire legal team and media advisors to help us navigate through the storm. To overcome the lies and conspiracy theories, we proved our authenticity and won a high-profile lawsuit. Instead of taking the trip to Disneyland, we chose to donate the money to charities and take a two-week healing trip to the Northern Territory.

This was a lifesaving trip where we experienced the healing power of culture through our legendary Yolngu elders and healers. We are forever grateful and will never forget this experience.

We travelled through the Territory, camping, fishing, hunting, and holding sacred ceremonies along the way, reminding us of how blessed we are to be a part of the oldest living culture in world history.

When you know who you are and where you come from, nothing can shake or break you, and that's the power that we possess as proud First Nations people, with a strong cultural identity.

The ancient wisdom and cultural knowledge shared by our elders has activated in me a deep sense of connection and humility. We have been blessed and humbled to make it through this together as well as we have.

The strength of family, culture and community has proven to be the super glue that has held us together at a time where we could have easily fallen apart and broken down – individually and collectively. Because of our strong support networks, we continue to pick ourselves up and go from strength to strength.

As a 40-year-old First Nations woman, mother and grandmother, I am finally at peace with my life. I am blessed to have had the best teachers in my parents, grandparents and godparents, who have all moulded me into the strong, resilient person I am today.

I am constantly reminded that 'nothing grows in your comfort zone', so I push myself to do my best every day – with clarity and sobriety. I want to live by example, so my children and grandchildren have a positive influence.

As I reflect on my life, I am reminded of all the trials I have overcome and know that my pain is not in vain. I share my story to encourage others who may be suffering in silence – as I did for way too long – to speak up. When we speak up, we take back our power and liberate ourselves.

In addition to my full-time job, I have various advocacy roles, including advocacy for greater protection for victims of bullying. In a Royal Commission, I called for 'Quaden's Law', but we need more than legal reform. We need a holistic approach, including teaching our children to be accepting and kind, as well as emotionally resilient.

As Quaden says, 'to not be rude and just be kind and nice'.

Quaden is now 12 years old, with maturity well beyond his age. His life experiences have shaped him into a strong, funny, smart, young man who fills me with a level of pride beyond words.

Without my struggles, I would not have found my inner strength, nor the power of gratitude. I wake up and give thanks for each new day that I spend with my children and grandchildren who bring so much joy.

Without my struggles, I would not have learnt how to swallow my pride and ask for help. If I continued to suffer in silence in fear of being judged and shamed, I would have sunken into deeper depression that would have eventually claimed my life. I encourage people to reach out and connect with support groups, or others you may know who have been in similar situations.

Keep an open mind and heart, making your healing journey top priority. Self-care is important. Have a 'happy place' to go to, or a hobby to enjoy that's easily accessible anytime you need to escape.

Pain is our biggest teacher. Ensure you take time to sit and process everything that comes up for you. You need to feel it, to heal it. It can take a lot of time and energy, especially if you've endured many traumas.

Be kind to yourself and surround yourself with positive people and resources.

When life gets too much, find an accountability partner and let them know when you're struggling – to ensure constant check-ins of your emotional and mental health.

Adopt a holistic approach and look after your mental, physical and spiritual wellbeing. This could include prayer/meditation, visualisation and positive affirmations/mantras, music, journaling, exercising, healthy eating, sleeping well and keeping well hydrated. Love and laughter are the best medicines, so fill your life with love and laugh out loud as often as you can.

Chapter 8

Under a Coolibah Tree

Hugh (Bill) O'Connor

**Rising from an accident that caused the loss of my leg,
then continuing to run a vast sheep station for 60 years.**

*'True character rises to the surface and
is revealed when under pressure.'*

In 1936, I was born in the most remote town in New South Wales – Tibooburra. My life before the accident was normal for a bush lad. A stint at boarding school, sport, particularly cricket, and plenty of hard work – fencing, mustering, stockwork, and trucking wool and stock throughout eastern Australia.

I lived and worked on the family-owned sheep and cattle station – 'Narriearra' – all my life, except for ten years when I worked for Uncle Hughie at Mt Poole station, near Milparinka. Being a young teenager when I began working at Mt Poole, the experience moulded my character and helped prepare me for future life events.

In 1962, when I was 26, I was the first in my family to get a pilot's licence, which changed the way we operated on the farm, and made our lives easier in many ways. We were all thrilled about this achievement and rightly celebrated.

However, that year was marked by another major event, one that we would not celebrate.

About six kilometres from the homestead in the Coolibah channels, I was preparing a fence site with my offsider, Ron Lazarus. As I guided the auger (post hole digger) to the place I wanted to put in a post, which was at the base of a tree, the auger hit an underground root and bounced back, catching a piece of old wire – and my left foot!

By the time Ron stopped the motor, my leg was wrapped around the auger and just about torn off.

'Get the pliers and cut me out,' I said.

'I can't look at it, Bill,' he replied.

'Go and get Dad,' I yelled.

Ron took off in the Land Rover, and I started to think more clearly. I was on my back with the sun shining straight into my face. I thought: *this is the wrong place to be*. Like Ron, I didn't want to look at my leg either, but I made myself and found two bits of wire hooked together over my ankle. By unhooking them, I managed to free my leg from the auger and crawl into the shade of a tree. I started getting thirsty, but there was more to think about than thirst. My thigh bone was sticking out of my leg, and with every beat of my heart, a stream of blood jetted out.

I had to stop it, or bleed to death. I removed my belt from my shorts and pulled it tightly around the stump. The blood kept coming, and I knew I was in real trouble.

My only other option was wire. I wound a piece of wire around my leg, pulled it to the top of the leg and twitched it. The blood stopped. To hold the bone up, out of the dirt, I put a stick under my damaged leg, over my other leg and over the post I was trying to dig the hole for. That kept the air flowing through.

Sitting there, waiting for help, I lit my pipe and had one draw. It tasted terrible, but oddly enough, I held onto the pipe and tin of tobacco tightly. Don't get me wrong, I wasn't having a picnic. All I wanted was to get onto an operating table and be put out of it.

Dad soon arrived and sent Ron to get my brother Jim, who was about 11 kilometres away at 'Connulpie Downs'. Dad had the shearers' stretcher and mattress alongside me when Jim arrived. I crab-crawled across to the bed with my right leg and two arms. Together, they lifted me on the stretcher and onto the back of the ute, and then they drove me back to the homestead.

Mum had already called the Flying Doctor. I would have been a bit of a mess for poor Mum. Jim suggested we take the wire off to save the leg by letting the blood drain down into the torn section. I agreed with the logic and removed the wire.

Jim gave me a dish to wash my hands. I'm not sure what this exercise was for. Maybe to stop me from frightening the doctor with all my blood.

The plane arrived and the pilot, Vic Cover, said to the doctor, 'We'll go straight to the Hill'.

The doctor replied, 'I don't think another half hour is going to make any difference to this.'

So, we landed at White Cliffs and collected a chap who had a badly burnt face and arms from removing the cap off a boiling radiator. We finally arrived at the hospital in Broken Hill.

I woke in hospital with very little feeling, if any. There was a half-moon structure holding the bed-cloth off my hips and upper legs. My left leg, of course, was the one I was worried about. And so, I moved my right leg over to where my left leg would be, but it wasn't there.

Knowing my injury intimately, I was not surprised by this revelation.

A nurse came in, and I said, 'I just got my pilot licence, and now they've cut my leg off.'

'You will have to see the doctor about that,' she replied.

I didn't need the doctor to tell me my leg was amputated. Nor did I need an argument. I went back to sleep.

The next morning, the surgeon told me that although my leg was amputated, I would be able to continue flying my plane, as I still had a good stump on my left leg.

This was wonderful news, but the thought remained on what to do through convalescence. The hospital was full of nurses to take care of me, so that problem was quickly solved.

I would stay for as long as I needed to heal. For six weeks, while using painkillers, I used the hospital as a sort of boarding house, coming and going as I pleased.

Once I was off the pain medication, it felt like a blow torch was aimed at my left foot – despite it no longer being there. The blow torch pain lasted for at least six months and has never completely disappeared. It's called 'phantom pain'. Six or more times a day, I experienced lightning strikes of pain down the phantom leg. After a while, I learnt to jam the stump against the bucket of the artificial leg to stop the pain from sweeping through my body and disorientating me.

Another strategy I used to cope with the pain was isolating it with my mind. By isolating the pain to one spot (by focusing), I was able to tolerate the pain without drugs. After a year or so, the severe pain gradually diminished in intensity and now rarely occurs.

My road to recovery had a few other obstructions. Namely, the reaction of some people to my new disability. Some, who thought my presence might wipe part of my disability onto them, would dodge me.

When loading something heavy onto a ute with people around, I don't ask for help. If it is offered, I might accept. Some people would offer to help without hesitation, but others seem to think that to get mixed up with a 'cripple' is not a good thing. Yet they're quite willing to help able-bodied people. Maybe they think they'll be 'stuck with a cripple' if they help. Whatever their reason, I learnt to be independent.

I also learnt that by accepting what I couldn't change, I could maintain my equilibrium. I couldn't change what happened to my leg. I couldn't change how some people behaved towards me.

But what I could do was shift my mind to things that I loved – my family, my work on the land and getting all my licences back, including my prized pilot's licence. These things gave me a sense of normality.

My family had mixed ideas of what they thought was best for me. My brothers wanted me to get a pension. Dad wanted me to be a publican in a Tibooburra hotel. However, I chose to stay on the land because I loved it and couldn't imagine any other life for me.

I'm 86 now and came through without a major mess to my business or career. I have achieved a lot in my lifetime. I ran the biggest single-owned station in New South Wales successfully for over 60 years, with a disability, and have now purchased another station with my son. I've travelled around Australia and overseas with my family. I have seven wonderful grandkids and an unquenchable thirst for knowledge. I now enjoy spending my days reading and learning new things, while still being out in the wide-open spaces.

I have come to realise that I am stronger than I thought, both in mind and body. Adversity, after all, challenges, shapes and strengthens us.

My advice to anyone in distress is to remain as calm as possible. This can be extremely difficult, but when you're calm, you think more clearly and make smarter decisions. Our mind is an amazing tool that can help or harm us. Learn to use it to your advantage.

About 70 years ago, I read *From Here to Eternity*, which is about a platoon of soldiers in the US army. There was a bully who always stood over someone, and a gentle soul, nicknamed Sister Mary, who looked after everyone. When they were on the frontline, in danger of being killed, the bully 'lost it' and Sister Mary threatened to shoot him if he didn't pull himself together.

This story stuck with me for two reasons. True character rises to the surface and is revealed when under pressure. Secondly, you need to get up and keep going, no matter what.

If I could offer one more piece of advice about life, it would be to follow a path that feels right for you, and don't let anything stop you.

Chapter 9
Sink or Swim

Gayle Shann

Rising from a farm accident that destroyed my arms.

'A woman is like a tea bag. It's not until you put her in hot water that you know how strong she is.'

Ironically, I was a fiercely independent young adult who didn't want to rely on anyone. I grew up on an isolated cattle property in north Queensland with three sisters. As we didn't have brothers, we learnt to do what many might consider men's jobs, from shoeing and breaking in horses to castrating calves and fencing – jobs that were integral to bush life.

I met Mac when I was 22 and he was 19. We had a strong connection right from the beginning, and within three years, we were married and managing my father's property in central Queensland – 'Cantaur Park' – 170 kilometres from Clermont. It needed a lot of work and kept us busy, but we loved every minute of it.

In 2002, when Mac and I had been married not quite three years, we had a friend, Adam Griffin, helping us build a fence around the homestead garden. Mac and I started digging the holes. Mac was operating the tractor, and I was shovelling the dirt away from the auger. My leather glove caught on a release pin and dragged me into the shaft of the digger.

Mac heard a thudding noise, and by the time he turned to look and kill the machine, it was too late. My body was a mangled mess. Mac presumed I was dead and ran inside to call 000. Adam, meanwhile, untangled me from the machine and carried me to the house. He then took the phone from Mac, freeing Mac to find me, following the trail of blood.

As he arrived, I was coming out of unconsciousness and asked him to move my right arm, which I thought was stuck up above my head. When he lifted the blanket, he saw a large black hole where my right arm, shoulder socket and my entire shoulder blade had been twisted off. From my arms, hands, fingers, legs, ribs, vertebra and nose to a large laceration across my face, my body was broken. Mac said my top eyelashes were on the top of my head and that half of my forehead was exposed. It couldn't have been a good look!

Knowing the severity of my injuries and the time it would take for help to arrive, I can only imagine the panic that must have set in for Mac, even if he didn't show it. The Royal Flying Doctor, a rescue helicopter and ambulance were all set in motion. Neighbours arrived, and a retired nurse began to implement first aid. Out of desperation to stop the bleeding, she clamped the blood vessels on my amputated side with her fingers while continuously communicating with the Flying Doctors heading our way.

About two hours later, the emergency services arrived and induced me into a coma to do some bush surgery on my gaping arm hole. Fearing the worst, Mac and my father were called in to say goodbye before I was flown to the Townsville Hospital.

Adam, meanwhile, volunteered to untangle what was left of my right arm from the tractor, and freeze it. It is quite amusing looking back because we had a discussion the night before about how weak in the stomach some people are when it comes to gory stuff. Adam confessed to being such a person, and there he was the next day doing the unthinkable.

Upon arrival in Townsville, I was screwed and bolted back together, then put in a coma for 52 hours. Waking up in hospital was a painful blur. When I first learnt of losing one arm, I thought I could eventually adapt and ride horses again. However, when I discovered that extensive nerve damage made my other arm useless, leaving me with *no* arms, it painted a whole different picture. Yet, in all honesty, I took the news well. No meltdown. Must have been the drugs!

Mac and my mother were by my side every day of my three months in hospital. Other family members were there on and off too and were my lifeline.

From Townsville, I was flown to Sydney where I experienced some of my darkest times coping with multiple, excruciating and complex surgeries. My weight dropped to 40 kilograms while enduring unrelenting neuropathic pain in my paralysed arm. They warned me it was coming, and boy it turned up with a vengeance. Apparently, the brain sends messages to your arm, and when it doesn't get a response, it presumes something is wrong and creates pain signals. When I later contacted other people who experience neuropathic pain, I was told I had joined the club that 'no one knows about, and no one wants to join'.

Finally, it was time to go home. In the grip of a terrible drought, it was a bitter-sweet experience. Many people encouraged us to move closer to town for easier access to help, but Mac and I had put so much hard yakka into setting our property up, we didn't want to walk away from all that we had done. I guess it was a case of sink or swim. I believed that all my previous experiences set me up to cope with this and, knowing I had great support, I chose to 'swim'.

I thought the hardest part would be not riding horses and working outdoors again, but I soon realised that day-to-day living, with no arms, was my focus. I relied on Mac for everything, from applying my makeup and dressing me, to cooking and feeding me. Another challenge was the weight of my paralysed arm hanging from a sling around my neck. It might be removed one day, as it restricts me in many ways, but there is always the possibility that some future technology might restore it.

During my second trip back down to Sydney for rehabilitation, they discovered a hole in my spinal cord that was leaking spinal fluid, or cerebrospinal fluid (CSF). Without sufficient fluid surrounding my brain, it sat on the base of my skull and, as you can imagine, caused incredible headaches. All I could do to relieve them was to lie flat. I had to lie down in some very peculiar places in the 12 months it took to rectify it with innovative neurosurgery.

For the first two years, sleeping was also a struggle, and both of us had little. However, dominating all these challenges was and continues to be the neuropathic pain. I try to distract myself from it and take high doses of medication. While the medication dulls the pain, it doesn't take it away and causes side effects and other problems. For example, it can't be taken while pregnant. Although we still have time to ponder whether to start a family or not, we realise it will be exceedingly difficult.

It's clear that I couldn't have managed this ordeal without my family, friends and, of course, Mac. I saw so many sad cases in hospital and rehab where people had no loved ones, or their partners left them post-accident. One thing I really learnt from this experience was the importance of family and how precious it was to have them with me. I'm infinitely grateful to Mac and my family, on both sides, for their love and support. Mac's life completely changed too, and there wouldn't be many husbands who do what he does. Mac is my strength and inspiration to stick around and have a fulfilling life.

My love of horses and cattle supported my recovery too. We love to breed and sell the best cattle and campdraft horses we possibly can and watch them compete and perform around Australia at a high level. Finding new stud calves and foals is the highlight of our year!

Adjusting to life after the accident was difficult, and it's not easy now, but I know there are a lot of people worse off than I am. I have a lot of things to be grateful for, and with that gratitude, I find strength and happiness every day.

Life is always hectic for us, but I guess that's the way we like it. Our lives revolve around improving Cantaur Park, which gives us passion and purpose. I go mustering on my 'four-wheeler' (motorbike), which two generous people modified for me. I do all the bookwork for our business by using a giant keyboard and rollerball mouse on the floor, using my toes. I also help in the cattle yards by using tabs on the gate sliders.

As soon as I accepted my injuries and changes to my lifestyle, I was grateful to be alive and seized the opportunity to have a good life despite the circumstances.

Resilience, I believe, is the key to adapting to whatever circumstances you face. Someone once told me, 'A woman is like a teabag. It's not until you put her in hot water, that you know how strong she is.'

We mightn't like to be referred to as tea bags, but I think it's true.

My advice to people in hardship is to not give up on what you want. Be thankful for what you have and don't dwell on what you don't. Seek the best help you can and throw yourself into your life's work or passion. Be patient, love those around you and appreciate everything you have.

Chapter 9

Chapter 10

#6Bs

Brad Millsteed

**Rising from depression and creating
a movement for men's health.**

*'Humans are "herd animals"
and stronger as a collective.'*

I'm a 50-year-old father, husband and farmer from Watheroo, in the mid-west of Western Australia. Like many men in my situation, my priorities are family, our farming operation and my community. Although the rewards are rich and irreplaceable, maintaining these priorities over time can be at a personal cost.

Life always throws challenges at you. Some are easier to manage than others. For me, being involved in team sports, like footy and cricket, helped me to reduce my stress and manage challenges when they rose. Sadly, male team sports gradually faded out in Watheroo, leaving a void for my mates and me. Our families were growing. Our businesses were growing. Being busier than ever before, we had less time for ourselves and no team sport, to play or support, to bring us together as a community.

In 2014, we tragically lost a 17-year-old nephew in a road accident caused by fatigue. He was like our godson, and his passing caused me and my family immense grief. Prior to this tragedy, there were other factors stemming from family and industry that incrementally added to my stress. It's often the case that it's not one cataclysmic episode that knocks you down, but a continued succession of smaller problems. We all know that if a paddock has too much stock pressure, the soil starts to drift away and erode, making the paddock sick and unproductive. For a while, I became sick and unproductive, depressed to the point of contemplating a one-way drive.

However, I decided that this would not be an option and, instead, I would be pro-active. My first step was a visit to my GP, who prescribed anti-depressants as a short-term solution while I built an ever-changing and evolving personal management plan with a counsellor.

Through self-education, I learnt more about grief and wellness. And it soon occurred to me that I wouldn't be the only bloke feeling this way. So, I was inspired to do more and be better for myself and others.

The year 2017 was a very dry year. For many city people, rain is an inconvenience. For farming people, it's critical to our financial and mental state. Without rain, a host of pressures build, both externally on the farm and internally in our minds, bodies and spirits.

In May that year, I received an email from the Movember Foundation promoting their 'M8 Day' on 8 May – it's a day to check in on a mate. We had some fallen trees in a paddock that had been tidied up for paddock preparation, so I decided to host a bonfire and BBQ for the local blokes on this day, to check in on them all.

I posted something on Twitter about it (@BradMillsteed) and ABC radio discovered it and invited me to have a chat. It was during this chat that the concept of #6Bs was formed: Blokes, BBQ, Bonfire, Beers, Bonding and Bullshit.

The event in Watheroo was a great success. #6Bs did more than fill the void of team sports, it encouraged blokes to get out and have some bloke time, some testosterone time, a time to connect in open conversation as a male community.

It was not disrespectful of our families, for they are precious. It was a way for blokes to be together, without the need to be the hunter-gatherer and protector of others. It was a safe place to just be a bloke and talk about bloke stuff, without fear of judgement or labels.

There must have been a need for it because other #6Bs events were held around Western Australia and later in South Australia. We even began connecting each event with a purpose – a farm tour, a butchering workshop, a cooking day – anything along those lines to give blokes a reason for the day, while also having bloke time.

In 2017, when #6Bs was conceived, I was struck by the significance of the number six. Back then, the stats relating to suicide in Australia showed that eight Australians lost their lives to suicide every day, and six of those were blokes. Six Aussie blokes every single day. So, #6Bs then became a tribute to the memory of the souls who couldn't fight the fight with their demons any longer. Unfortunately, that statistic has worsened. Presently, nine Australians commit suicide daily, with seven being blokes. Every death to suicide is a preventable tragedy, and I hope that with growing awareness and other nationwide initiatives, we will make a difference and significantly drop this number.

In 2018, #6Bs was awarded by an agricultural company and given a small bursary with which we developed our logo and brand. I had also found some enamel pannikins (metal cups) and thought they were a lot like us blokes – tough and strong on the outside, yet when we get bumped, dropped and knocked, chips come off. Regardless of the damage, we're still usable and loveable. So, I had 100 of these pannikins made as gifts for people who had supported #6Bs. This soon led to an unexpected demand for the cups across Australia, and the world!

In the ABC's *Man Up* series by Gus Worland, it was identified that most blokes only have two mates that they will share everything with. That is on average. Some have more. Some have less. I now realise how important it is to have these mates, and to talk things through with them often, to prevent the little things from building up.

I have several Gotcha4Life mates and, much like an advisory board, as they all have different skill sets, I rely on them at different times in different circumstances for advice. I also share my wins with them, large or small. I've learnt the importance of acknowledging and celebrating life's wins regardless of their significance. These mates are a critical part of my personal management plan, along with #6Bs.

Civilisations have grown and prospered with the passing of knowledge between generations. With diminishing regional and remote populations, as reflected by the demise of team sports and closure of pubs, this has become harder to achieve, and not everyone likes sport or pubs. We need other ways to reconnect our generations to reinvigorate and strengthen our communities.

#6Bs has shown the power of bonfires. I am yet to find someone who doesn't enjoy sitting around a bonfire. Maybe we have an innate, primal connection with fires, or maybe we're attracted to the neutrality of bonfires. I don't know why, but no one sits around a microwave yarning with their mates, do they?

Blokes are renowned for not going to their doctors regularly. The open chats we have at #6Bs give a level of reassurance that it's ok to visit your doctor to get something checked or get help. We are fortunate to live in this modern world with access to professional help and medicine. If need be, we can have medicine to help balance our body's chemicals and aid our thinking and perception to allow us to build a long-term personal wellness plan.

It's reassuring to hear others talk at #6Bs about how their bodies have changed as they age, about their lumps and bumps and how parts don't always work like they used to. The chats normalise our common concerns and experiences. And they're not always serious. Often, our chats are light-hearted and fun. Sometimes, all we need is a good laugh.

It is important for blokes to know what makes them whole, spiritually, and not necessarily in the religious way. It's important to do the things that make us happy and content. For this reason, I have a happy Sunday ritual. I wash our car and ute, mow our lawn, then play in the kitchen to satisfy my #cockylikestocook hobby. Cooking something delicious with lots of love, for those I love, gives me great joy.

My life today is far better than it has been. I have learnt that I am Brad Millsteed first and foremost. Then I am a husband, father, farmer, and then a community member. My various roles are now balanced with care for myself.

I was dubbed a Men's Mental Health *Agvocate*. (Advocate, but due to my agricultural background: *Agvocate*!) However, it's not the notoriety that gives me satisfaction. It's making a little bit of difference to the lives of other men and, indirectly, to their families and communities, that really makes me happy, all thanks to an idea.

Agriculture is an amazing and unique industry. We are open to sharing our successes and failures with others in our industry ... and love it! Unlike many other industries, we don't protect our knowledge in fear of competition and this, I believe, is one of our greatest strengths.

I encourage men to share our *personal* wins and losses, just as we share our professional wins and losses. Hearing how others deal with similar issues can be very reassuring. Likewise, hearing about changes that made other people's lives better can be motivating.

We wouldn't drive past a mate's farm and see an outbreak of weeds in a paddock, or livestock in his crop without ringing him up to make sure he knew about it. The same can be said when a mate begins withdrawing from his regular activities and life. We need to notice that and not be shy to touch base with him to make sure he is ok.

Withdrawal is often the first public sign that people are not at ease with themselves. When the fight is starting internally, it's often difficult to reach out. It's often easier, however, for others to reach in. We need to empower more people to reach in and help their mates. Humans are 'herd animals' and are stronger as a collective. Even the most introverted loners still embrace the opportunity to interact with other humans.

I am just trying to be a better man today than I was yesterday. I hope that #6Bs will expedite generational change in the perception of men's health and wellbeing, so that the generations of men to follow us can live a little easier and freer in their own skin with less stigma and 'attitude' attached to being a modern man.

Chapter 11

Let's Talk

Jetha Devapura

Rising from obsessive compulsive disorder.

'Find your purpose by finding what makes you feel good, that also makes others feel good. When others feel good, you feel good in abundance.'

Growing up in Sri Lanka, I was the youngest of four kids. In 1978, when I was 12, we moved to Melbourne for a better life and education. My mother was a nurse, and having 25 percent white blood meant we had no issues coming to Australia under the then White Australia policy.

My parents told me that an astrologer had said that one of us four kids would do something special. Being high-spirited and confident, I assumed it would be me. Afterall, who else would it be! I am forever grateful for my parents for sharing that with me. It gave me a sense of certainty and confidence. Upon reflection, it also taught me how vulnerable children are to the power of our words. As a parent today, I choose the words I say to my children with great care to uplift them.

High school was fun and carefree compared to the strict schools in Sri Lanka. I could count the number of South-East Asian kids at the school on one hand. One day, two boys asked me 'Where did you park your elephant?' Without hesitation, I replied, 'The same place you parked your kangaroo.' I didn't see that as racism, as I didn't even know what racism meant. They were merely making fun of our differences, and I gave as good as I got.

In my teen years, I took on a part-time job selling newspapers at the Royal Melbourne Hospital. I proudly walked the wards shouting out, '*Herald* ... the final! Read all about it!' During this time, I was diagnosed with temporal lobe epilepsy after my family found me on the floor having a seizure. However, with the safety and support of my family, this didn't particularly phase me.

In the 90s, I became an engineer and took on a two-year expat assignment in Kuala Lumpur, Malaysia. This was a pivotal point in my life, as I discovered – the hard way – that isolation wasn't something I handled well. For the first time, I was alone, in a foreign country with a stressful job.

I wasn't equipped with the emotional tools to handle being away from family and friends, and my natural drive, confidence and level of certainty were slowly eroding away. I remember getting up one night and staring through my bedroom window onto the empty street that was thousands of kilometres from home. I would go back to sleep and hold my own hands for comfort.

As loneliness and uncertainty crept in, they opened the door to anxiety. With a 'brave-face' mask, pride kept me there for the full two years.

I returned to Melbourne half the man I was before my expat experience and was soon diagnosed with obsessive compulsive disorder (OCD). At times, the anxiety that drove the compulsiveness was so overwhelming that it felt like it dragged me by the scruff of my neck and made sure I kept checking the same thing that I had checked ten times already. With OCD, the anxiety will physically hurt you and mentally torment you until you get your fix of checking it again and again. One time, I remember the anxiety being so strong that sweat was running down my leg while I was sitting down.

After three months on Prozac for the anxiety, I started to feel better and stopped the medication. I kept my mental illness a secret, as I was embarrassed by it. I didn't choose to suffer in silence, but at the time, I didn't know any other option.

I then joined Nestle as an engineer and later moved to the country town of Echuca, in Victoria. As if I hadn't learnt my lesson already, I put myself in isolation once again, living alone there. My drive to achieve surpassed my fear of isolation. It was a high-pressure job where I had to endure an industrial lockdown and disgruntled factory workers. Coming home to an empty house day after day, away from my family, I relapsed for the second time.

Waking up to anxiety wasn't nice. It was crap. Like the first episode, I took medication for about three months to take the edge off. To this day, the thought does cross my mind if and when a third relapse will occur. However, I now have more tools to prevent it.

My journey to non-drug recovery started when I returned to Melbourne where a fridge magnet in a shop caught my eye. It was a 'virtues' card about courage, which signalled a powerful message that I needed courage to manage my OCD. I needed courage to say NO to compulsive checking. My fear was about not getting things right or perfect. There were many times I would start cooking, then throw out the food, wash the pan and start again. If I didn't do this, I sometimes feared I could hurt someone, or in some cases, even kill them. I would tell myself repeatedly that I had the courage to not keep checking and that it was ok.

Telling myself 'Jetha, it's ok' led me to a deeper discovery of self-compassion.

I had a great role model in my dad, who was an extremely compassionate man. Anyone who knew my dad would say he was a true gentleman and a kind man. He supported orphanages in Sri Lanka and many charities here in Australia. My mum, on the other hand, demonstrated true courage to be the pioneer who came to Australia alone, started work, got an apartment for us and organised schooling for the kids. I feel that as Mum passed on her genes of courage, my dad passed on his genes of compassion to me. All I knew about self-compassion then was that I needed to be kinder to myself during the grips of anxiety.

Both courage and compassion slowly started working for me, and then I discovered commitment. I knew that I needed commitment to back myself up and persevere through the uncertainty. Commitment seems to come naturally to me with my perfectionist mindset and inbuilt determination. People say Taurus people are stubborn. I say they are determined. I now had three virtues that gave me wings as a non-drug therapy to manage my OCD.

Did they work all the time? No. However, they were the foundation of feeling better about myself from the inside, and it was only the starting point.

A holiday to Sri Lanka changed my life. It gave me the perfect scenario to practise, test and grow my foundation of courage, compassion and commitment. Although I had been to Sri Lanka several times since migrating, this trip was different. It was the first time I visited the National Cancer Institute (NCI) in Colombo.

'Why are these mothers and their children on the floor?' I asked.

'Oh, they are floor patients,' came the reply.

I soon discovered there was no proper transit home facilities for outpatients who came to this 800-bed Institute. Many outpatients who knew no one in Colombo, or who couldn't afford the bus trips back and forth for their chemo or radiation treatments, or who were simply too weak to travel, slept in the corridors of the Institute's wards. Some carers would sleep under the beds of their children to be with them. I simply couldn't walk away from this. In First-World hospitals, this would be untenable.

The word compassion in Latin means 'to suffer together'. Although I saw the suffering of the children and the adults with cancer, I had a shield of detachment that didn't leave any room for pity, but rather compassion to act and do something about it. And that I did.

In 2003, I founded the Courage Compassion and Commitment (CCC) Foundation Australia Inc. and, thanks to an amazing team of volunteers in Australia and Sri Lanka, we raised over 1.6 million dollars to build the largest cancer transit home in Sri Lanka comprising of 194 beds. We call it the CCChouse. Today, no child, adult or carer sleeps on the floor at the NCI. We provide everyone who stays with us a home away from home for as long as it takes for their treatment, at no charge.

At the time of naming the charity, I used the three virtues that were closest to my heart and have guided me to manage my OCD. Courage to say NO to the compulsiveness. Compassion to be kind to myself. And Commitment to keep fighting. These three virtues have become my foundation and identity.

In late 2000, I was looking for a change from my corporate life and wanted to make a difference here in Australia. I felt I was doing a lot in Sri Lanka and wanted to do the same in Australia. Along came Interchange Victoria, a not-for-profit charity providing respite for families with children with a disability. I loved the work but faced financial strain, following a $200,000 loan to a friend. After returning only $20,000, he later filed for bankruptcy. During this time, I moved back to my parents' house, as I wasn't earning enough to pay my expenses and a mortgage, which now had an additional $180,000 on it.

Although financial losses like this can really bring people and families down, I was determined to recover, and I clearly remember how I did this – in minutes.

In the midst of my frustration and helplessness, I walked into my parents' bathroom, looked in the mirror and told myself that everything happens for a reason and there was a good reason for this too. Sure, my current situation made me move back in with my parents, who were now in their late 70s, but they loved having me there!

So, I asked myself to focus on the comfort, companionship and joy I gave my parents by being there with them. From that moment onwards, my mindset shifted from 'victim', to 'serving' my parents. I felt so relieved and free. I learnt the power of letting go and looking for the good in every situation. It cost me $180,000, but the lesson was priceless.

My interest in mental health grew, and I discovered that the suicide rate in Sri Lanka was among the highest in the world. Since we had already copied and pasted the Ronald McDonald House concept, I thought why not copy and paste Lifeline to Sri Lanka. A couple of phone calls to Lifeline and a meeting with the then President of Lifeline International, Mary Parsissons, saw the establishment of the first Lifeline Centre in Sri Lanka in 2009. We call it CCCline. Today, 12 years on, CCCline receives more calls than any other similar crisis support service in Sri Lanka. We are saving lives.

As my understanding of mental health increased, I was able to cope with my OCD much better. I realised that by applying my virtues of courage, compassion and commitment through my charity work, I had switched from a 'me focus' to a 'we focus', thereby diverting my emotional energy, which would otherwise render me helpless, towards helping others. I converted my 'strain' to my 'strength'.

The more I understood why people call the Lifeline service in Sri Lanka, the closer I got to understanding suicide prevention. Among the top five reasons why people call Lifeline in Sri Lanka, three of them can very easily affect any of us at any time: relationship issues, economic pressures, and loneliness.

From this, an important question emerged for me. Why do people bypass their family, friends, colleagues etc. (their village), to speak to a crisis supporter on the other side of the line that they would never see or meet?

The answer was clear. People are fearful of being judged, ignored, humiliated and punished. All these reasons fall under three universal fears of not being loved, not belonging and not being good enough. The very same fears that kept me from talking about my OCD for years. I had struck a root cause as to why a small worry, not addressed, could escalate into a bigger issue, including mental illness or suicide.

This realisation led me to founding the Let'sTALK Program in 2016, which is now in schools and organisations in Australia.

Mental illness can touch anyone at any time. A fundamental preventative measure is to create an environment of psychological safety at home, school, workplace and in our community, by allowing people to raise their voices to share ideas and mistakes without the fear of being judged, ignored, humiliated, or punished.

Today, I am stronger, more confident and feel like I am alleviating suffering in our world. My wife, Erica, is my greatest supporter, and my two girls, Jasmine-Jade and Emerald-Rose, inspire me. When I look back at my journey so far, it started with great certainty and confidence that dipped into the depths of uncertainty and anxiety. As I reached those depths, I was able to reach out and gather some gems that helped me to feel more comfortable with uncertainty and to let go of most of my anxiety.

Here are some of the gems that serve me:

- **Uncertainty is a gift of growth.** Get comfortable with being uncomfortable by trying something new, different, or challenging once is a while.

- **Uncertainty can lead to anxiety if you let it.** If it's under your control or influence, do something about it. If it's not, then let it go, but check that your expectations are real.

- **Anxiety is an important message that should be opened, read and addressed.** The best way to get rid of anxiety is to know what to address (important mail) and what to throw in the bin (junk mail).

- **Resilience is how well you bounce back** as well as how well you let the crap bounce off you.

- **Find your purpose** by finding what makes you feel good, and that also makes others feel good. When others feel good, you feel good in abundance.

- **Find your gifts** and nurture them. Find your gaps and step into them. Your character develops when you embrace both your gifts and gaps.

- **Do one thing vulnerable every day.** You will find your ground and inspire others by being the real you.

- **Go for self-compassion,** not just self-esteem. One is an inside job, and the other is an outside job. The inside job will always be there for you when you fall.

- **Leaders need to understand that psychological safety** is key to igniting creativity and growth. The best way to build psychological safety is to make people feel seen, heard and valued.

- **Talk about your worries,** mental illness, or even suicidal thoughts. As much as you may be scared to lose those who may judge you, losing yourself is not an option. You will be pleasantly surprised by how many people care about you, even strangers. You are unique and rare and there is no other one like you on this planet. You are worth it.

Human connection and relationships are fundamental to our mental wellbeing. A simple conversation can be the difference between an ending or a beginning. Let's make it a beginning.

Chapter 11

Chapter 12

The Show Goes On

Ann Ballinger

**Rising from grief, while managing
our outback sheep station.**

*'At the end of the day, I had to accept
my loss and get on with my life.'*

Bill and I were married in 1981. He was 31 and I was thirty. We were late starters, and I think both sides of the family were relieved that we had found suitable lifelong partners. We shared a love of the bush and interest in people. I handled the small talk, and Bill wanted to help and be their saviour! This strong, sensitive, ambitious, sophisticated bushman with beautiful cursive handwriting and old-fashioned character will always be my hero.

I was delighted to be getting married, making our home and family in the bush, starting a garden from scratch, and doing everything ourselves. Most of our furniture was from someone's dump, but a coat of paint or lacquer goes a long way! With two young daughters, our early marriage was a blissful time of my life.

Nothing is permanent, however, and in 1986, I lost my dear mother and mentor to cancer. My father was heart-broken and died later that year. We moved to a 'bigger and better' property near Longreach, and Bill's mental health began to decline. Starting with doubt about his decision to move, his subconscious mind took control and threw logic out the window. The day we arrived at Jedburgh on a hot droughty day, Bill's world, and therefore my world, came tumbling down.

Jedburgh was 360,000 acres of Barcoo River country. It was getting dry, and water was scarce. Gloom and negativity filled Bill's mind. He eventually went to a GP, who gave him medication, but he felt shame about taking it. He didn't want to go anywhere or see anyone, and on one occasion when a neighbour called, he hid. Only after a lot of coaxing, did he come out and enjoy a meal with us. As his mood swings and anxiety intensified, I concealed all the guns, although he never talked about suicide.

Living in isolation makes men and women resilient, but this stoicism can sometimes get in the way of seeking help when you need it. After owning Jedburgh for just 12 months, we sold it and headed to the Sunshine Coast. However, Bill's anxiety and fear of losing our money continued. In good faith, family and friends would ask how Bill was, but unless they had experienced mental illness, few people could understand it.

For the first time, Bill was admitted to a psychiatric ward in hospital. I was relieved that he was safe, and I could have a break from the pressure. This was a turning point in Bill's illness, but unfortunately in the wrong way. Bill couldn't tune into any sort of wavelength with this psychologist, who led us to believe that Bill was odd. Fortunately, we found a more suitable psychologist who helped us realise that there were many people suffering from depression. He was not alone in his illness. This revelation was comforting and gave us hope.

Around this time, in 1988, our son Rupert was born. We were delighted to have a healthy baby boy but, under the strain of a newborn, my coping mechanism fell apart and unfortunately so did Bill's. For the first and only time in the 20 years we were married, I told Bill that I didn't have the strength to endure anymore. From that moment, Bill transformed into a responsible and wonderful husband again. He even did the washing! We always credit Rupert's birth as one of the triggers for kickstarting his life again.

In the same year, the land inevitably called us back out west, and we moved to Stockholm, a 30,000-acre property near Longreach. Bill was on a high, too high in fact. As though making up for lost time, he was open and wanted to tell the world about what he had been through. His vigour, vitality and confidence were firing on all cylinders. We bought an old Cessna plane to seed the country with buffel grass. And soon, Bill was known as 'Buffel Bill'; he put the plane to work and seeded over a million acres across western Queensland.

Bill then became involved in agripolitics, and everyone wanted to hear what he had to say. The social intercourse energised him, and through his years of flying, he knew Western Queensland from the air like the back of his hand. A Godly type of persona was developing and yet, at the same time, Stockholm was neglected. And there were other tell-tale signs that not all was well for Bill. He was overweight, snoring and had sleep apnoea.

One evening in 2000, Bill and I sat in the garden having a drink while our teenage kids – Bella, Rupert and Winnie – were playing tennis with their friends. There was lots of fun and laughter, and I mentioned to Bill that it really didn't get much better than this.

However, as I had learnt before, nothing was permanent.

By the next morning, 'Mr Gloom' had returned, and I felt despair and helpless.

It was the Sydney Olympics and Cathy Freeman was racing – an unforgettable night for all the wrong reasons. Bill was in a manic state while we sat on the veranda waiting for an ambulance. He ended up in a psychiatric hospital, where he was anxious, pale, drawn and unshaven. We spent days discussing how he had got to this point, and that in his eyes, I was often the reason it had all gone wrong. He expressed a negative and selfish attitude, which I suspect was connected to his survival instinct.

Our family united at Stockholm again for Christmas, but little did we know, it would be the last time.

Chapter 12

Christmas Day passed quietly and tensely, but the show had to go on. It was 'crutching time', and the children and I were preparing the sheep. At sunrise on Boxing Day, Bella, Rupert and I went mustering. Someone always stayed with Bill, and as Winnie loved to sleep in, it was her turn. At about 9 am, Winnie called on the two-way radio to say that something had happened to Dad. The rest of the day was a blur. Bill died that morning of a heart attack.

I psychoanalysed this journey many times, talked to people, read articles and books, felt guilt for all the things I could have said or should have done, but at the end of the day I had to accept my loss and get on with my life. I stayed on Stockholm mainly because I loved the work and the life. It enabled security and familiarity in a supportive community. Despite many people telling me to sell the property, staying at Stockholm wasn't a difficult decision.

My children were a wonderful comfort to me. Bella stayed with me for the first year when a lot of talking, crying and comforting took place. For two years, I wallowed in grief, contemplating how to create my new life. Sometimes, I was overwhelmed with decision-making. What do I need? What do I like? What do I dislike? What are my strengths and weaknesses? How do I manage these with work? And to be honest, I didn't always make the right decisions, but I came to terms with the outcomes and tried again to get it right. When I made mistakes, I forgave myself. Self-forgiveness was a necessary part of my healing.

Working on Stockholm gave me purpose and satisfaction. I knew that Bill was still with me in spirit and would be proud of my constant maintenance and improvement of the place – with help from others sometimes, of course. The job also involved managing up to 11,000 sheep and a couple of hundred cattle. This huge responsibility helped me to focus, yet it wasn't easy.

When it rained, the dirt roads became impassable, so there'd be times when I wouldn't see another person for six weeks. Although often alone physically, my friends and family would call frequently to stay in touch. One friend was always available to discuss management strategies and was a touchstone to help me make decisions. Another would help me with mechanics, another with mustering etc. I will never forget their support, nor underestimate the value of a good community.

The increase of dingos and wild dogs made sheep management tough. There were times when I'd find big, healthy ewes with a hole in their side where a dog had ripped their kidneys out and left the poor things standing. I remember the desperation I felt as I shot them.

I recall the distant sound of barking dogs one night; it was a dreaded sound because I knew they were attacking sheep. I grabbed my gun, rushed to the Toyota and headed out. I found the sheep, but the dogs had disappeared. In my haste to save the sheep, I became hopelessly bogged and had to walk four kilometres back home in the dark, in my nighty!

I eventually sold all my sheep and stocked only cattle.

In western Queensland, rain is seldom a problem. Droughts were more prevalent, and 2002 and 2003 were particularly tough. Sometimes, when I'd run out of water at the house, I'd have to fix the pump at the dam. The frustration of not being able to fix what I needed to fix was sometimes unbearable. One day, I hurled the spanners in the air and yelled at Bill for not being there to help me. After two years of 'wallowing', I decided that I couldn't go on like that. In a clear and decisive moment, I said to myself, 'I've got to get over this and enjoy myself again.'

And I did.

By thinking positively, I was able to find peace and contentment with my life after Bill. I held on tightly to wonderful memories of our life together, the greatest of which are raising our three perfectly imperfect children of whom I am proud. Rather than focusing on what I had lost, I scanned for reasons to be grateful – the rain, the healthy stock (when not in drought), my friends and family, the sunsets, my veranda, garden, dogs, and of course my own good health. Appreciating even the smallest things, such as a nice cup of tea, would give me joy. There are always reasons to be grateful when you look for them.

Eighteen years lapsed and, given that none of the children wanted to live on the property, I decided the challenge was over and it was time to retire. I moved to the Sunshine Coast and am happy living here among many friends, new and old, from the bush. My involvement in agricultural committees and boards is rewarding, and I enjoy walking and getting to the beach when I can. I have a wonderful relationship with my three children and grandchildren. We live our own lives, and at my 70th birthday recently, one of my daughters thanked me for being me, so they could be themselves – a legacy I inherited from *my* mother.

My advice to people who are struggling with depression is to reach out for help, but selectively. Reach out to family and friends who you can trust and who understand mental illness. Be frank and speak your mind. They won't judge you, and most people do want to help. Don't waste your time and energy talking to people who 'don't get it'.

It's true that time heals. When I was grieving for Bill for the first two years, I called it 'going into suspension' and I needed that suspension to accept the reality and adapt to life without him, with confidence and hope. That suspension enabled me to clear my mind. Only with a clear mind was I able to prioritise my work and personal life and make prudent decisions.

We can't control what happens to us, but we do have choices in how we deal with what happens. Regardless of your losses, your health and wellbeing benefit if you think positively and choose contentment.

Chapter 12

Chapter 13

Getting the Job Done

Brent Mickleberg MP

Rising from PTSD as a returned soldier.

'I returned to finance, and rather than living in "life and death" moments on operations, I was writing loans in a bank.'

We are indeed a product of our upbringing. My early adult years saw me following the path of each of my parents. My mother's family were graziers and drovers with a strong connection to the bush. I grew up with stories of stock camps, stations, rogue bulls and brown snakes. I inherited a love of animals and, after further inspiration from reading *The Cattle King*, I headed to the bush as a Northern Territory stockman in pursuit of a career in the beef industry. Sitting around the campfire one night, I realised that this was not the way to buy my own station. I needed to switch to a more lucrative, albeit less satisfying career in finance.

My father served as an Infantry Officer in the Australian Army for over 40 years. Like many who have been raised in a military family, it was only a matter of time before I felt compelled to serve alongside my father. I joined the army in 2004 and soon learnt that service in the military is more than just a job. It is a way of life. As a soldier, you value mateship, loyalty, teamwork, commitment, service before self-interest, high standards of behaviour, and have a clear sense of right and wrong.

Military service took me to countries far less fortunate than ours. In Afghanistan, I worked as an infantry captain attached to a US Special Operations unit and was lucky enough to work alongside our coalition partners. I never felt I was going to die in Afghanistan, but I often felt vulnerable.

Driving was always stressful. I constantly scanned for threats while driving past locals going about their daily business. I recall one incident when we were in a small, two-vehicle patrol and one of our vehicles got bogged. We received reports of Taliban radio chatter discussing our predicament and were very exposed. I remember a US convoy driving past and leaving us out there. In the end, it was an Afghan Army truck driver who bravely stopped to help. I will never forget how my heart raced as I bent down in front of him to do up the tow chain. In the end, he was just a Good Samaritan helping a fellow soldier.

I can't speak in detail about my service in Afghanistan, but some of the things that we saw will stay with me for life – images of children killed by the Taliban, suicide bomb attacks, and US soldiers killed by Afghan soldiers they had been mentoring. For me, the hardest part was seeing women and kids traumatised as well as the vulnerable exploited by the Taliban. All too often, young girls and the mentally ill were coerced into conducting suicide bombing attacks on coalition forces and Afghan authorities.

Over time, perceiving everything as a potential threat becomes normal. Often, the tension felt before an incident was more intense than the incident itself. Layers of unreleased tension begin to have a debilitating effect over time. I liken the pressure that builds over time to filling a bath with water. If you don't drain the bath, the pressure builds into anxiety, feelings of isolation and anger, and it ultimately brings about conditions such as PTSD and depression.

In 2013, I returned to Australia. My wife Anna arranged for us to go on a cruise. It turned out that trapping me on a boat with 2000 people for a week was not such a great idea. I found myself being hypervigilant and aggressive. And being close to others meant that I was constantly on edge.

It was difficult adjusting back to civilian life. I eventually returned to finance, and rather than living in 'life and death' moments on operations, I was writing loans in a bank. I felt alone, unfulfilled and had a yearning to return to Afghanistan.

Had I been offered deployment back there, I would have jumped on a plane in a heartbeat. Most civilians do not understand why soldiers want to deploy. Just like footballers who want to play a game of football to apply their fitness and skills from training, soldiers want to deploy so that they can apply their training and be out there standing shoulder to shoulder with their mates in the harshest of environments and not let them down. Soldiers also want to serve because of an attachment to that identity. If I wasn't a soldier, I was nothing meaningful.

My struggle continued. Images and nightmares kept returning, and my anger grew. Driving was one of the hardest things to adapt to, as I was constantly scanning for threats. Over time, I started to consider ending my life so that I would not be a burden to Anna or my family. I felt that I was not doing anything to make their lives better anyway. The only thing stopping me was the hurt that I would inflict on Anna and my family.

As my isolation and anger grew, Anna began to realise that I needed intervention, and one afternoon, she cancelled her shift to stay by my side. In hindsight, I know that her decision to stay home that day saved me from doing something more drastic. It was her intervention that gave me the strength to seek treatment from a veterans' counselling service. It was a difficult time for our marriage, and I am blessed that Anna stuck with me and helped me recover. Anna was and continues to be my anchor.

In 2015, we had our first child, Lara. Up until Lara's birth, I craved to return to Afghanistan to do some meaningful work as part of a team and experience the adrenaline that comes with it, but with the birth of Lara, I learnt that caring for a child more than satisfied that urge. Lara's birth changed my focus and gave me a new sense of purpose. Nothing is more important than my family. I will never let my job define me again.

My family and counselling support were major factors that led to my recovery, but that wasn't all. I sometimes relieved my stress by going out to our farm. I found it relaxing to 'hang out' with my cattle in the paddock. I find the peace and tranquillity inherent with animals and nature therapeutic.

During this time, I was involved with the Liberal National Party (LNP) as a volunteer and was invited to run as a state Member of Parliament. The role appealed to me, as I believe in putting my hand up to get the job done, rather than just complaining from the sidelines. Thanks to a united and massive effort by many people, I was successfully elected as the LNP member for Buderim. In 2018, I delivered my maiden speech in parliament, which included my struggle with depression and PTSD. Sharing my story in public for the first time was not easy, but it was cathartic. It gave me a sense of relief and release from the stigma I had attached to it.

It was also an opportunity to bring awareness to the experiences of many other war veterans and their families. Too few people are willing to stand up and tell their stories. I want my children to know that they should not be afraid to seek help if they ever need it.

I now have the great fortune of a rewarding professional and personal life. I have four healthy children and serve a wonderful community. At work, I find the small triumphs the most satisfying – the small wins that change lives, but few people see.

My advice to others who are struggling with mental health is to seek help. Swallow your pride if necessary and reach out. Containing it within yourself does not help you or the people around you. As the saying goes, a problem shared is a problem halved. No one will turn you away. Be honest with yourself and acknowledge you have a problem, then take action and address and overcome it. I was lucky to have Anna in my life to prompt me to take those steps. If I can do it, so can you.

Chapter 13

Chapter 14
Sailing for Solace

James Prascevic

Rising from PTSD as a returned soldier.

'They would get up on the bow and re-enact the scene from Titanic with their arms splayed out feeling the breeze in their face.'

At the age of 22, I was a qualified plumber, had been paying off a house from the age of 17 and had my own sub-contracting business. I was doing everything that I set out to achieve by the age of 30, and I thought: *is this my life?*

So, I decided to challenge myself and become a frontline soldier. In April 2002, I joined the Australian Army. After many months of training, I marched into the 1st Battalion in Townsville. There I served for almost ten years and was lucky to deploy to East Timor, Iraq and Afghanistan. I completed the Commando Selection and Training Course, as well as other Special Forces courses before breaking my ankle and injuring my back in a parachuting accident.

Unfortunately, this was the start of the downfall of my military career, and 18 months later, I separated from my wife and was medically discharged from the army with the 'ankle of a 90-year-old', failing back health, tinnitus, anxiety, major depression, and post-traumatic stress disorder (PTSD). I returned to my 'hometown' of Lorne, in Victoria, existing day to day, and wishing I wouldn't wake up in the morning. I couldn't see a future, nor anything to look forward to – and I didn't care. I wished that my parents, who owned the house next door, would give me their permission to give up.

After a failed attempted suicide, I was determined to 'get it right' the next time. However, my three-kilogram silky Maltese dog, Joey, put a stop to that plan! Whenever I was down, she would look at me with concern, so I decided to put her down before taking my own life. The next day, I woke up to those little brown, helpless eyes looking at me again and couldn't possibly go through with the plan. Instead, I chose to fight on until the night-time, when the process would begin again.

Some people say it's selfish to take your own life, but unless they have been there, they will never understand the feeling. The emptiness you experience, and not being able to see a future is so real, it's the only thing that made sense.

I didn't trust myself with the pills in my house, so my mother managed my medication, dispensing around 20 pills a day. I also talked to a local psychologist weekly for almost ten years before she retired, and a psychiatrist who I still see 12 years later. Luckily for me, my psychiatrist worked in a psychiatric hospital where I would spend a lot of time over a period of about eight years. Every few months, I would spend a few weeks there to recharge and reset myself.

I did have some enjoyment in my life. I had my parents, Joey, and an amazing view of Bass Strait from my house. I could also see the Lorne Pier from my chair in the loungeroom. Being close to the ocean made me more comfortable, and I would stare at it for hours and feel somewhat at peace.

I started to go to the pier each day and fish for hours, just as I had done as a kid. I enjoyed watching the fishing boats launch behind the pier and decided I wanted my own boat and go out onto the ocean. I found a 4.45-metre tinny and would spend hours out on the water. Even if I didn't catch many fish, my only thought was the end of the rod. I honestly felt 110 percent better, mentally and physically. However, this peace of mind was temporary. At night-time, I would drink, as my demons would catch up with me.

So, I decided I needed a project to keep myself occupied at night.

One day, while out fishing, I said to a mate, 'I wonder if I could get this thing (referring to my boat) to Tassie?'

He said I was mad, and I replied, 'That's exactly the response I wanted!'

I yearned for a project. No, more than a project … I yearned for a challenge and thought it would be a great idea to do this for a mental health charity. I was soon approved to raise funds for the Black Dog Institute, which is a not-for-profit organisation for diagnosis, treatment and prevention of mental health conditions, including depression and anxiety.

Six months later, I set out from Lorne and crossed Bass Strait in my little boat, then returned home in it six days later. I raised thousands of dollars for the Institute and, more importantly, awareness for mental health.

I then focused on my next challenge, which was writing a book about my life experiences and how they affected my mental health. By recalling and reflecting on what happened in my life, writing the book helped me grieve and accept my circumstances.

After months of persistence, I finally found a company to publish my book: *Returned Soldier. My battles: Timor, Iraq, Afghanistan, Depression and Post-Traumatic Stress Disorder.* Just before my book was published, I started sailing at my local sailing club and doing my Yachtmaster Course (for which I would qualify a few years later).

Not long after I started sailing, I purchased the first of three boats I would own. During this time, I was also lucky to be part of two races, including the 2014 Sydney to Hobart yacht race on a Volvo 60. Ocean racing and being part of a crew reminded me of the army – out in the good and bad weather, working hard, getting sunburnt or soaking wet with little or no sleep, but going through it together and being able to enjoy a drink, in moderation, and talk about the hard and miserable times we shared. Like in the army, we dealt with the challenges together, and we relied on each other to keep things going and found strength through our comradery.

Around the time that I discovered my love of sailing, I also discovered my future wife, Wendy. After swearing I would never marry again, our first date for a coffee on the waterfront, which lasted for three hours, soon changed my mind.

Experiencing the mental and physical benefits of being on the water and sailing, I wanted to help other people suffering from depression and PTSD. I started taking out sailing former soldiers, first responders, as well as personnel who had been affected by addiction. They would get up on the bow and re-enact the scene from *Titanic* with their arms splayed out feeling the breeze in their face. I would teach them to set the sails, read the wind and steer the boat. I enjoyed sharing what I loved to do, and they truly appreciated my time.

Having a purpose, goals and a water environment helped me mentally, and so I decided to look for a new challenge. Searching the internet for sailing, I found a British website called the World Speed Sailing Council. They listed and recorded sailing records for teams, two-handed and single-handed, across different bodies of water around the world. The solo aspect interested me, as I revelled in it, so I looked at what was achievable.

The one that spiked my interest was the record from Sydney to Auckland. It had been set as a team but not as a solo. My boat was not the fastest, so I thought if I could finish the passage, I could be a Sailing World Record Holder. Even if I could hold the record for one day, I would be over the moon!

So, I started preparing myself and my boat for what would be my first ocean crossing. After a year and a half, I was ready and sailed the boat two-handed from Geelong to Sydney in January 2020. A few days later, I left Sydney, sailing solo for what was meant to be an eight-day trip. After being becalmed for several days in mid-ocean, I finally arrived in Auckland 12 days later – exhausted and relieved.

I had achieved my goal. I was a Sailing World Record Holder. Just before I sailed into Auckland, I said on video that this would be one of my proudest times, but not long after I returned home, I felt that what I had achieved was insignificant. Underpinning this feeling was my unfulfilled goals as a soldier before I was medically discharged. To overcome this, I try to set more goals for myself and keep looking forward.

During my second solo Tasman trip, I decided I needed a change and to lessen the pressure of being a solo skipper and owner. I decided to sell my boat upon my return and get into ocean racing. And I did just that and managed to join a 50-foot race boat.

In my spare time, I go camping and gold detecting in the bush, which I love. As of July 2021, I am happily married, paying off a house in Geelong, and I take minimal medication. The idea now is to help as many people as I can by telling my story and how the ocean has helped me. If I can help one person not go down the track I did, by sharing my story, then I will be happy.

My advice to anyone who is suffering from mental illness is to seek help, ask for any assistance available to you, find your passion, set small goals and work towards them each day.

Chapter 14

Chapter 15
Lost at Sea

Louise Eacott

**Rising from the loss of my family at
sea on *Great Expectations*.**

'Don't let anything stop you.'

I grew up in a sailing family when female crew was rare. My stepfather and brother would race most weekends from the Brighton Yacht Club, and I'd be invited only when they needed extra weight. We lived comfortably in Melbourne in an apartment above my mother's hair salon.

My father moved to Queensland and began a new family. Had I not gone to visit my father to celebrate his baby's first birthday, I may not be alive today.

In December 1989, my stepfather (Graham Baldwin), 16-year-old brother (Bryan) and crew set off for the Melbourne to Devonport sailing race on Graham's yacht, *Great Expectations*. While I was in Queensland, my mother, some family friends and our miniature dachshund (Heidi) flew down after the race to celebrate with them.

On 4 January 1990, they all set off together across Bass Strait to return to Melbourne. According to a witness, millpond seas in Bass Strait turned rough the day after they set sail. The entire vessel and crew of six were never seen again.

I can't remember the moment I heard the news, but I remember seeing my father when he heard it. We were in a caravan park where he lived, and the caretaker came with the phone. Our friend Julie was on the other end with the news. After getting off the call, my father looked over to me with a face white with fear … and the rest is a blur.

My father, stepmother and baby brother packed up and drove non-stop for 21 hours down to Melbourne. I sat in the backseat pacifying my baby brother all way. I was only 14 at the time and didn't have keys to Mum's salon or apartment. I had to break into our empty home. I remember the phone ringing constantly from media, sympathetic clients, and family friends.

Chapter 15

After the sea searches stopped, hurtful conspiracy theories emerged. My father decided to block me from media exposure. We closed my mother's business and our money quickly dried up. My father took us back up to Queensland to begin a new life in a caravan park.

It was tough. My bedroom was an awning beside the caravan, and the rudimentary hot-water system was either too cold or burning hot! Nothing in between! Adjusting to my new school was hard. Known as a 'caravan kid', there was no way of overcoming that stigma. The permanence of my new situation struck me one day when I was buying shoes with Dad. Mum had always bought Adidas shoes; however, all Dad could afford were runners from Kmart.

I realised then that my mother, brother, stepfather, family pet, friends and life as I had known were gone forever.

How did I cope? Being adaptable helped. Accepting what you can't change and going with the flow. Caring for my baby brother also helped a lot. I've always loved kids, so nurturing and nourishing him helped me to nourish myself. I also dived into study and focused on books. I grew up quickly then and decided that if I worked hard, I could take charge of my life and be successful. Refusing to never feel sorry for myself, I decided to never define myself as a victim of this event.

On the contrary, I feel lucky. I'm lucky to be alive and lucky for all the good fortune that has come into my life. Regardless of your situation, there are always reasons to feel lucky and grateful.

I believe that if you do the right thing, good things come to you. They may not come straight away, but they always come. I'm now blessed with a loving husband, who shares my values, and four wonderful children.

One of my sons lost $10 from his pocket recently. He was upset, but the next day he helped a neighbour remove a dead possum from her garden. Much to his delight, he was kindly rewarded with $10 from the neighbour. Kindness leads to kindness. I've always tried to do to others what I would like done for me ... and I don't expect anything in return. I give because I want to give, not for any expectation from the receiver.

My mother taught me to not limit myself. Don't let anything get in your way, she'd say. That determination served me well. I put myself through a Fine Arts degree in university by delivering pizzas at night.

Driven by my love of family, I worked hard and built a successful corporate career, enabling my father and 'baby' brother and their families to live nearby. We have established new roots on a hobby farm in a coastal area of Melbourne and enjoy a comfortable, secure family life.

Genuine connections with people are also important to me. I like to be honest and open with people and surround myself with like-minded, positive people. I dislike hearing people talk about their continual bad luck, and I prefer to think positively and move on from the past.

A rewarding part of my corporate work has been mentoring young people. I encourage people to not let the stigma of their past hold them back from their future. Live without boundaries, and don't be afraid to ask for help. Most people are kind and *want* to help. If a friend, family member or colleague expressed their vulnerability and asked you for help, you'd want to help them. It makes you feel good to help. It's human nature. So, if you need help, you're not a burden. People genuinely care about you. Ask for help.

Chapter 15

Chapter 16

A Northern Territory Love Story

Bill Brayshaw

Rising from the stolen generation, Cyclone Tracy, and the loss of our son.

'We can't change what has happened, and if we accept that, we don't churn ourselves up by wanting something else.'

W̌e're a couple who've had a hard-working life, not a hard life. Aileen was born in 1940 on Manbulloo cattle station near Katherine. We don't know for sure which year it was because there are no records of her birth, but we thought 1940 sounded good. I was born in Brisbane in 1937, but neither of us spent our childhood in a way that our parents intended.

In 1942, when Aileen was about two years old, the government took her from her mother because she was 'coloured'. Aileen's mother (Kabunga) was Aboriginal, and her father (Ben Ahwon) was a Chinese station cook. Aileen was too young to remember being taken away, but she does remember being told that her mother died and that she had a new home. The truth, however, was that Aileen's mother died years later (exact time is unknown) and they never saw each other again.

For a few years, Aileen lived in Katherine with the District Welfare Supervisor, Ron Ryan, and his wife. They were kind and cared for Aileen. When Aileen was about seven years old, she was sent to Melville Island to be raised by the nuns. Aileen recalls that they too were mostly kind, and she called her favourite nun 'Mum'.

It was a regimented life for the kids on Melville Island, where calmness, independence and respect were instilled. Mind you, education was a low priority, resulting in Aileen having a low literacy level, but the children had time to play and have fun. Aileen fondly remembers sometimes camping with the nuns and making good friends with the other girls, who were much like sisters. She describes the experience with a peaceful acceptance. There was no point complaining or being upset about it. That was life.

At the same time Aileen was living far away from her mother, I was a young lad also living without mine. My mother died in 1942 while giving birth to my baby sister when I was aged five. My father was in the air force and was away during the war, so my four siblings and I were raised by my grandmother on a dairy farm near Narrabri in New South Wales.

My grandmother, Ivy May Brayshaw, was a hard-working woman. As a widow, she was managing the farm and taking care of five kids, including a newborn baby. The farm didn't have electricity, so the cows were milked by hand, and all our clothes were washed by hand. She wasn't a soft, cuddly grandmother, but she provided everything we needed.

After milking the cows every morning, it was my job to deliver the milk around the town on a cart pulled by a horse. It had to be done early because the milk wasn't refrigerated. When that was done, I'd walk two kilometres to school. I was *always* late. After school, I'd have to get back home quickly and do the milking and milk-run all over again. I did that seven days a week for many years.

I found time to play, of course.

'Get outside and play,' my grandmother used to say. 'You know you're not allowed in the house!'

One cold morning, our cat climbed into the wood oven to keep warm. Unfortunately, a Polish refugee who stayed with us during the war was unfamiliar with our cat's habits and closed the oven door. He stoked the fire and headed out to the dairy, unaware that he was cooking our cat! We were all upset when we discovered the dead cat. However, my grandmother watched my reaction, and I distinctly remember it was the first time that I decided to accept whatever was to happen in my life. We can't change what has happened, and if we accept that, we don't churn ourselves up by wanting something else.

Aileen has the same approach to life. She finds peace by accepting what has happened instead of resisting it. The government's philosophy that underpinned their welfare policy was terrible. They believed the black people would eventually disappear and that the people of mixed colour required removal and government care. Nonetheless, Aileen doesn't see herself as a 'victim' of the stolen generation. It happened a long time ago and belongs in the past. This peaceful acceptance of 'what is' has served us well through all our challenges.

As a young man who loved adventure and the bush, I headed to the Northern Territory; this was where I met my beautiful Aileen. I was a taxi driver in Darwin and remember the first time I saw her. Wearing a red-petticoated skirt and red shoes, I thought: *wow, what a beautiful woman*. I was captivated by her cheerful smile and beautiful nature. I know I use the word beautiful a lot when I talk about Aileen, because she really is, inside and out.

We married in 1960. Only three people came to our wedding, because we didn't have any money then. Two days after our wedding, I was sent to Lajamanu (Hooker Creek, as it was called then) to do carpentry work. I stayed there for three months to earn enough money to buy our first house in Darwin (with a government loan).

From then on, Aileen and I worked hard, side by side, growing our family and our financial security. Aileen was a full-time mother for our three sons, while I worked in the Darwin fire brigade. We built six houses ourselves, and I mean every part of our houses. From the foundations to the roof top and the furniture inside, Aileen inspired me and helped me with everything.

Some people used to tell us to go away for holidays instead of working so hard. 'Life's too short', they'd say! But Aileen and I enjoyed our hard work. We loved working together and building our financial security. It was rewarding. Much of our financial security can be attributed to our property development project in Darwin. It took us ten years to get council approvals for the subdivision, but our patience and perseverance paid off.

Patience and perseverance have been valuable virtues in our lives. They helped us manage one of the main problems stemming from Aileen's childhood – the absence of her birth records. The government at the time had a 'Stud Book' in which all Aboriginal kids of the stolen generation were recorded. However, there was no record of Aileen in the Stud Book, which caused a great deal of angst when we later tried to get a driver's licence and passport for Aileen. It was as though she didn't exist. Standing in the Office of Births, Deaths and Marriages with Aileen, I said, 'Here she is. You solve the problem.' While we eventually procured proof of her existence, it was one of the most frustrating challenges arising from that government intervention.

When Cyclone Tracy hit Darwin hard in 1974, we all crouched down in the bathroom, huddling together as it blasted through the night. Our roof was blown away, and I remember thinking: hell, our workmanship won't look good after this! When the sun rose the next day (on Christmas morning), we looked out across Darwin and saw that all the houses had been flattened. Our house was one of the few that remained. The cyclone took Aileen's wedding dress, but we were lucky.

About 70 people were killed that night. There was only one undertaker in town and not enough coffins. Being in the fire brigade, I helped to find the bodies, wrap them in blankets and bury them. A year or so later, we had to exhume some of the bodies to send back to their families in America and interstate.

One of the hardest times we've faced was the death of our son, Mark. Aged 52, he died suddenly of a blood clot, which caused a heart attack. It was a shocking and sad time for our family, but again, nothing can change what happened. You accept it and look forward.

We now have four grandchildren and two great-grandchildren and a wonderful life. We've been married for 61 years, and I've loved Aileen every single day. We cuddle each other 50 times a day. Sometimes, when I'm in my workshop, I think about Aileen, then put down my tools and go inside for a cuddle, then return to my workshop. We love fishing and spend six months every year camping in our secret place in the Top End. We both have a strong connection to that country.

How our sons raise their families is up to them, but we hope that they teach them what we have taught our boys – the importance of looking ahead and knowing that whatever you're going through, it will pass. Find peace with whatever has happened, look ahead and love.

Chapter 16

Chapter 17

My Healing Cocoon

Antonia Kotsiros

Rising from Parkinson's disease.

'Being mindful, playful and focusing on elevated emotions plays a big role in healing.'

My life felt complete. I was happy in a 22-year relationship. I had a loving family, a full life and financial security. I worked in the music industry and then in the coffee industry, creating coffee brands and outlets, as well as operating a luxury accommodation business with my life and business partner. Then something happened that changed my life completely.

In 2007, I was diagnosed with Parkinson's disease, just after my 40th birthday. I felt shocked, bewildered, sad, defeated, and worried about my future. My mind, body and soul felt heavily burdened.

My partner and I had philosophical differences about how to manage the disease. My partner wanted me to go on the traditional path of taking medication. However, I knew that there were many areas of my lifestyle that could have contributed to this diagnosis, so I was more interested in taking a holistic approach and getting to the root cause.

During my investigation, my tests showed that I had a high level of heavy metal toxicity. I consequently 'detoxed' and eliminated most of the heavy metals. To my great relief, this resulted in diminishing neurological symptoms, and I wanted to take my detox programme further.

I undertook a series of infra-red sauna sessions. Unfortunately, I didn't drink enough water during this time, and I became dehydrated and developed kidney stones. This was misdiagnosed as a 'UTI', and I was given five different courses of antibiotics in the space of two weeks. This was the beginning of my serious and fast health demise.

As my health was declining, my partner did not believe that the effects of the antibiotics were damaging, and she held on to the belief that I was in denial about the Parkinson's diagnosis. As things got worse, my partner took control of our businesses, looked after the house, cooked, assisted me, and looked after the dogs. This imbalance of input caused a rift between us and, despite trying to make it work, our relationship ended in 2015.

During this time, I was emotionally, psychologically and physically frail. I started using a walking frame, became reclusive and needed 24-hour care. I had mixed emotions about the break-up. There was a part of me that felt sadness, yet there was another part of me that felt relieved. I felt like I could now begin my healing without the pressure of feeling guilty, or of being a burden. However, my confidence and self-esteem had plummeted, and I felt like I had a very big mountain to climb. I was unsure how to begin this climb, but I knew that no one else was going to do it for me. My wellness was my responsibility.

So, I began the climb, one step at a time.

Ongoing counselling helped to restore my emotional and psychological state, and I realised that I needed more support. For two years, my parents cooked and delivered food to me daily. My best friend, Lisa, was also an amazing support. Lisa checked on me daily and helped me secure carers through the NDIS.

I retreated from my outside world and left my house only 20 times in one year. I retreated into, what felt like, a healing cocoon. From the outside, it looked like I was depressed. However, in my cocoon, along with the pain, there was a richness, colour, texture, and a spirited commitment to heal. Even in my darkest, lowest points, there was always a voice that delivered a message: 'It's ok. This is your "seasoning" of life experiences that teaches you how to feel compassion when you serve others.' This felt comforting and gave me my 'why' – my reason for this experience.

When I hit rock bottom, I began looking for lessons in the experience. It was almost like a natural meditative state that made me the *observer* of my body, rather than being *in* my body as a victim. These lessons are hard to explain. It was like I had insight and wisdom. For example, rather than feel angry, scared, resentful etc., in those difficult moments, I felt compassion, tenacious, and I had a vision of myself supporting others because of the experience.

A counsellor recommended the healing work of Dr Joe Dispenza. This was life-changing, not only because I had access to profound healing methods and testimonials, but I now had scientific evidence that you can heal your body and mind from many conditions. I always had an intuitive feeling that this was the case. However, I came across a lot of opposition to this belief which, through unconscious conditioning, discouraged me to follow these possibilities.

With my strengthened belief in the innate power of our mind and body, I committed myself to a self-healing journey. I became more mindful of having good nutrition. I began meditating and doing 'breath work'. Through these practices, I became stronger and stronger. I continued to heal without taking medication. Over two years, I gained more independence and mobility, which meant I no longer needed 24-hour care.

I let go of feelings of hurt and made space for elevated emotions such as compassion and gratitude for all that my partner did to support us in the last five years we had together.

There are many lessons and gifts that I have acquired through my journey. One of the most helpful is that, to heal, you need to have the mindset that you are not a memory of your past, but the vision of your future self, the person you want to be. I let go of thinking of who I was and what I had become. I felt strong and excited about the future. I committed completely to my transformation, and then everything started to change.

I have found that being mindful, playful and focusing on elevated emotions plays a big role in healing. I believe that it is important to be aware of a diagnosis. However, it is equally as important to not wear the label as your identity. I have always had healing in my sights, so I have never said, 'I have Parkinson's'. Instead, I say, 'I was diagnosed with Parkinson's'. There is a significant difference.

I have now reduced the need for carer assistance significantly as I continue to restore my health. I feel more confident, more creative, positive, centred, and passionate about projects I am immersed in. I am rolling out a video business, launching a book to help people who have been diagnosed with Parkinson's, writing a script for a documentary about my healing journey, releasing songs on YouTube and developing an online course about the importance of mindset for healing and an abundant life.

I am loving the way my new life and purpose are evolving and can't wait to help others become the best version of themselves, despite their adversity.

Chapter 18

Don't Judge a Book by its Cover

Dianne Moussa

Dealing with blindness, a spinal disease and constant physical pain.

'I'm a woman on a mission to prove that nothing is impossible.'

Hi, my name is Dianne. I'm 39 years old and legally blind. However, there is more to me than meets the eye. This is my story …

Like a typical Sydney girl, I hadn't a care in the world! I was the second youngest of six kids, with Lebanese parents who worked hard to provide for us. I remember many long summer days at the beach with my family. They were such fun times spent running along the beach and making sandcastles. I loved to dance, draw and was the life of the party, the one who'd get everyone up and moving.

However, when I was 11, my world turned upside down.

I remember walking out of a cousin's house late one evening. I couldn't see a thing and yelled out to my mother, 'I can't see!'

'Stop mucking around,' Mum said. 'You have school tomorrow.'

With no understanding of what was going on, Mum grabbed my hand and I climbed into the car. The next day, my vision was still strangely poor and continued to gradually diminish. An eye doctor referred me to the Prince of Wales Hospital, where I was poked and prodded. I then discovered I had an eye disease called Retinitis Pigmentosa (RP). The first sign of RP is loss of night vision. There is no cure, I was told, and I'd be blind by the time I was forty.

I remember coming home and watching my mother crawl up on the couch. She was simply undone by the news; it's a memory I will never forget. The other adults in my world were sad and quiet.

Little did any of us know that things were about to get a whole lot worse.

Only three months later, while getting ready for school, my mother came into the bathroom to pass me a towel. She noticed a lump on my back. 'Come straight home today,' she said. 'We're going to the doctor.'

That afternoon, I was taken to a doctor who thought I was just carrying my school bag incorrectly. Nothing that a few good stretches wouldn't fix! In a week, the lump grew bigger, and my mother demanded a referral to a specialist. I was soon with Australia's leading spinal surgeon and was diagnosed with a severe spinal condition called scoliosis. It required correction by the removal of nearly eight kilograms of ligament and tissue from my spine. I underwent major surgery, which came with the risk of ending up in a wheelchair.

I had the operation and spent two and a half months flat on my back, while my spinal cord healed. The pain was excruciating. I remember my dear mother sitting on a chair beside me for 24 hours every day. Then began the hard work of standing up again. When I eventually mastered standing, I was fitted with a special fibreglass brace that was worn under my clothing from the moment I woke up until the time I would go to sleep.

With help from my family, I learnt how to walk again. I remember holding onto Mum's hand and putting literally one foot in front of the other and forcing my feet to move. And I had to get moving, as I was about to start high school!

My high school days began while losing my sight and wearing clothing four times bigger than my body to fit over the brace! Puberty and bullying soon hit and, needless to say, my high school days were challenging. The hardest part was being put down by people in authority. I remember sitting with my mother in the principal's office and being told that I wouldn't amount to much. I heard similar words as often as a baked dinner. Other times, I was put down by people in less obvious ways, such as by their tone or behaviour, but their message was the same.

My parents' Lebanese culture heightened their concern for me. With little prospect of getting married or having children and living with disabilities, it was a triple whammy, and my parents were fearlessly protective of me. With the best intentions, they felt it was not necessary to continue school after year ten. However, this was a case of 'agreeing to disagree'.

When you lose your vision, you lose a lot of other things in your life that sighted people take for granted – for example, you miss visual social cues. Often people don't know how to approach you, and it's therefore harder to develop new relationships. You become isolated. Funnily enough, the COVID lockdowns made little difference to my life.

So, I had an important choice to make. Do I bow to people's low expectations of me and my life, or prove them wrong?

I consciously chose the latter. A fire was ignited in my core. I was not going to sit in a corner and waste away. Not me! I was determined to have a normal and independent life just like everyone else. I didn't know how, but I knew I would.

Everyone around me buried themselves in their own grief and no one outlined to me what was happening. From somewhere deep within, my spirit rose, as did my need to know more about life. I started asking lots of questions and made the decision to learn as much as I could. My determination enabled me to learn how to live independently, work hard, travel the globe, and embrace life's adventures.

Even though I am now legally blind, have nerve damage from the spinal surgery and live every day with pain, I stay positive and always find reasons for joy. Often, it's the smallest things that I treasure each day. It could be catching up with a friend, sitting by the ocean, listening to music, or sipping a good cup of coffee. I *savour* these moments.

I throw myself into life, often putting myself in the deep end. It's an attitude of 'jump first, then figure it out later'. I'm sure as hell not going to miss out on any more life. Enough is enough. Friends have said to me that I don't do life by halves and that I get things done. I guess there's some truth to that. I believe that time is of the essence, and I love to make the most of it.

I take responsibility for my life and back my own decisions – physically, mentally, emotionally and financially. I have always known throughout my life that I had to be the one to make it happen. I knew that no one else was going to make it happen for me. For example, I wanted a Higher School Certificate (HSC), so I worked for it over four years. Mind you, I have deep gratitude for the people who have come into my life and have travelled the course at various times along my journey.

I like to invest in myself and explore how I can be the best version of myself and have a positive impact on other people's lives. I attend self-development conferences, and in 2019, I was blessed to meet a global personal development icon, Tony Robbins, after being chosen to share my story in front of 2500 people. It was a life-changing event that propelled me into a commitment to constantly learn and focus on self-development. One of the greatest lessons I have learnt from Tony's work is that life hasn't happened to me. Life has happened *for* me. Looking back, I truly understand that all that I have endured has been for my benefit.

My faith also helps me. I know that without the grace of God's love, provision, protection, wisdom and guidance in my life, I wouldn't be the woman I am today. I wouldn't have had the opportunities, nor the strength to get through some of the hardest and darkest times in my life. Without the grace of God, I wouldn't be sitting here writing this story to share with you. I am incredibly thankful that when the human spirit has failed me, God's spirit has always been with me to lean on. My relationship with God is not perfect. Some days I ask him where He is, but mostly He is my peace, joy and strength.

A sense of humour has been a valuable tool throughout my life, including through the hard times. Laughter is often a better reaction to situations than being upset. Joy is like a good medicine.

In 2020, I travelled to Germany for eye treatment involving electrical stimulation. I was given a special exemption to leave Australia during those crazy COVID times. Unfortunately, while having treatment, I was locked out of Australia and that was a whole other journey in itself! But, like every other day, I put one foot in front of the other.

In 2021, I began full time study in massage with a goal of opening my own practice. However, the increasing pain of advanced osteoarthritis in my spine closed that door. Although it was disappointing at the time, I find that if you have a go at something and it doesn't work out the way you expect, it doesn't mean you have failed. It's better to have tried than not try at all.

Ironically, although my spine is damaged and inflexible, my flexibility to adapt to changing circumstances has been another key to my resilience. Although I had to walk away from helping people through massage, it hasn't stopped me from helping people in other ways.

I am now a Welfare Officer for the Senior's United Party of Australia. I work in a federal team to support the members on a personal level, ensuring that they feel heard and valued in our walls of parliament. Being of service to others gives me great satisfaction and motivation.

Regardless of our personal challenges, we can all contribute to society. It's about taking our eyes off ourselves, being grateful for what we have and being there for our fellow brothers and sisters.

I say to you, please don't take your life (or your senses) for granted. Open your eyes and ears and mind and heart and spirit to those around you because we don't know what each day is going to present to us. You never know what's around the corner. Rise up and take life by the horns without regrets. I don't want to die wondering what could have been, and I hope you won't either.

I'm a woman on a mission to prove that nothing is impossible. What's your mission?

Chapter 19

The Gifts of Adversity

Steven Farrugia

Rising from sexual abuse and Crohn's disease.

'The gifts of adversity give you a lens of resilience that carries you through life and expands your soul.'

I grew up in a migrant family in a low socio-economic part of Melbourne. We had a good family unit, and from a young age, I was drawn to martial arts and nature. Self-discipline and fast, unconventional learning were innate. Although my high school was tough and riddled with bullying, I managed that with relative ease. In fact, the hostile culture taught me some valuable life navigation skills.

I faced my hardest challenge when I was nine. There were a lot of kids in the area, and we'd often play together on the streets. There was an older boy who sexually abused several children in our street, and my sister and I also fell victim to his abuse. Being young, I didn't understand what was going on. I was confused and fearful, not only for myself, but for my sister, who I wanted to protect.

I didn't speak up because of the shame and disempowerment I felt, followed closely by guilt for not speaking up! My fear, shame, disempowerment, and guilt about the abuse were soon intensified by another layer of distress. My mother innocently made a comment that many gay people were contracting AIDs and dying. In my nine-year-old mind, I was therefore going to die! For a long time after the event, I lived with that belief and prayed for my life.

The belief eventually dissolved, but that experience reframed my world. I looked at the world with a sense of mortality, through the lens of a dying young boy. Everything that was important to me in life became crystal clear. And the gift of this experience was a deep appreciation of the present, of where I am now, as opposed to reliving the abuse. Often people relive their past traumas in their mind. I chose not to. I unconsciously cultivated a deep sense of gratitude for the experience, as it allowed me to discover the power of purpose, presence and mindset, which has served me well throughout my life and allowed me to coach and guide countless others, many of whom are executives of large organisations. Gratitude, I learnt, turns whatever you have into 'enough', and it allows your character to shine with its strengths.

The abuse empowered me to handle other challenges. Every other challenge I have faced since then has been through the lens of resilience. The experience motivated me and made me determined to never be disempowered again. I developed strength of spirit, mind and body through diving deeply into meditation, and educating myself in engineering and martial arts. My practice means I have strength in all aspects of life, which over time allowed for mastery in strategy, leadership, culture, innovation, entrepreneurship, and continuous improvement.

Another challenge for me was mild visual dyslexia. Reading is always difficult, but I can see an extraordinary world of patterns, which give me advantages in mathematics and business. My dyslexia taught me the value of embracing our differences. The greatest innovations and advancements in humanity come from people who don't fit the norms – Tesla and Einstein, for example. I call them 'outliers'. They don't have disabilities. They have *special* abilities. We can harness our differences, our uniqueness to create meaningful impact and evolution.

I also had Crohn's disease, a chronic digestive tract disorder that is regarded as incurable. I took symptom-relief medication, which led to depression, so I decided to cure it myself. I sat with *why* I had the disease. And I had an epiphany .... My father also had Crohn's disease, and I realised that I wished it upon myself, to relieve my father of it. I created it

– emotionally, spiritually and energetically, so I knew that I could clear it the same way.

Through the practise of self-healing modalities, including Brian Weiss' early and past life regression therapy and high-energy light vibrational frequency meditation healing technique, I was able to free myself from what is listed as an incurable disease. A year after starting my routine of healing, I was tested and the disease was gone, completely!

Through self-evolution, and assisted by psychologists, I was able to make sense of and see clarity about my life. I realised that connecting to your purpose is key to a successful life. Early on, before I started my business, I had a vision of succeeding and pledged that once I reached the milestone of one million dollars, I'd commit those funds to making a meaningful impact on humanity.

My personal purpose is to create a fairer world where every person has the opportunity to realise their full potential. To that end, I created a charity organisation called ShareTree.

ShareTree educates, engages and empowers altruistic individuals and businesses, while fostering a high-performance culture centred on gratitude. The enterprise was born out of the obvious lack of income equity globally. Almost 44 percent of the world's wealth and income is held by less than one percent of the population. At the root of all the limitations to people's opportunities to meet their fullest potential is a lack of 'enough'. In a tribe of 100 people, this would never occur – one person taking almost half the entire tribe's efforts to produce – yet this occurs in the larger tribe of humanity. Why is this?

My dream is for every person to have a sense of enough, so they can live with purpose and give their unique gifts to the world for the betterment of our planet and its dwellers. Imagine if everyone had the freedom to live with purpose. Once one has enough then their focus shifts from survival to fulfilment, and eventually purpose rises to the forefront of life's focus.

My advice to people who are facing adversity is to face it head on – with your purpose and character. Summon your courage to confront the issue and grow your character. Grow your soul. Be clear on your purpose, centred in your being and focused on where you are heading. When you're purposeful, centred and focused, the negative, critical people fall aside and, in that space, you attract people who are on similar journeys, those who will inspire and uplift you.

Reflect upon what gifts come from your adversities. There are always gifts if you look for them. The gifts of adversity give you a lens of resilience that carries you through life and expands your soul. Growth can only come from strain, so do not flea or fear it.

Be present where you are now and do not turn back to your traumas, rather see them as gifts to your growth.

Lead your life, personal and professional, with integrity and passion. Love what you do so at the end of your days, when you reflect on life, you will look not at how much you made, but how much you've made a difference.

Chapter 20
Warrior Woman

Carolyn

**Rising from the sexual assault of my children
and witnessing a horse massacre.**

*'Resilience is about finding your inner warrior and
calling on your inner strengths to guide you through
your own healing, and then the healing of others.'*

Prior to 2002, we lived a wonderful life with our three children on a magical 20-acre property in rural Victoria. We filled the land with a few horses, rescued sheep, chickens and even guinea pigs. Hubby supported us all, working hard in the dental industry, and life was great. I was outgoing, learning karate and living the country dream.

Then my world stopped.

Our eldest son, who was eight years old at the time, disclosed horrific sexual abuse that he endured by people known and trusted by our family. As the details came out of his mouth, my head was racing with thoughts of tearing these people apart, limb by limb. We took our son to a trauma psychologist, and she suggested I ask our other two children whether they had also been abused. I was mortified, as I hadn't even considered it possible.

I dutifully took the two girls aside and asked non-leading questions. Their responses were horrifying. And so began a long journey of healing.

I had studied shamanic healing in the United States and applied every 'trick' I learnt to help my children work their way through their rage, grief, anger, denial … the whole lot. Meanwhile, I put my own healing on hold.

In 2006, I became a volunteer firefighter. I think I needed to know I had the courage to 'fight fire', just as I needed courage to deal with my kids' abuse.

As we slowly came out of the fog in 2010, we joined a horse rescue organisation. I was trained to inspect neglect cases and enjoyed being a voice for the voiceless and making a difference for these beautiful animals.

In 2011, another atrocity occurred. Two hundred and eighty starving ponies were reported to the authorities, who gave the owner a year to fix the problem. Suddenly, a year changed to a week. All ponies remaining on the property after a week were to be shot. With my daughter and a handful of friends, we drove to the property to rescue as many ponies as possible. Having never been handled or trained, this was no easy feat. Miraculously, we managed to take 143 of them to safety.

Then came the four-day massacre, an event that is incongruent to the standards Australians would deem acceptable to any animal. We couldn't stop the shooting, but we could record it to expose the cruelty. As I ran from tree to tree with my camera, the shooters drove around in utes, shooting the terrified ponies. Some ponies took four shots to drop them. I ran to as many as I could to take photos of the random bullet wounds.

They say horses can't cry, but what I saw broke my heart. As they ran for their lives, some of the mares aborted their foals. We found a blind foal and desperately tried to rescue her, but the hired guns spotted her and rounded her up on their horses. Tragically, she followed the noises of their hooves into a killing pen.

These four days nearly broke me. I knew that I could either let part of me die with the poor souls or rise above it and make good from bad. From that moment, I vowed to start my own horse rescue organisation and honour the memory of the massacred ponies.

In 2013, the Winged Horse Equine Welfare was founded and is constantly growing, with hundreds of horse rescues and public support. Among the herd is a little mare called Tess, who we rescued before the massacre. Tess's recovery, from starvation and separation from her family, helped my recovery from the violence and suffering I witnessed. Tess is safe now and forever protected. The neglect and violence that her herd endured has not been in vain.

In 2018, another tragedy struck. Our beautiful family friend, Maddi, was killed on her hire bike in New York, while on the trip of a lifetime. Maddi was a 23-year-old psychology graduate, with the whole world at her feet. Her loss rippled across our hearts.

I flew over to New York to honour Maddi and support her family. Maddi died on the road where the New York marathon finishes in Central Park. I wasn't a runner, but I suddenly felt compelled to one day run the New York marathon in Maddi's honour.

However, I gained 25 kilograms since discovering the kids' abuse. I was told it was subconscious protection from the world. It took 16 years before I was ready to shed that protection. I began walk-run-walking, and then I managed to run a few kilometres. A snake bite to my leg in 2019 put an end to running for a few months, as did a disease of my thyroid in 2020. But despite the setbacks, I'm alive, and my dream lives on.

Aged 56, I made one of the best decisions in my life. I engaged an extraordinary running coach to help me not only become an athlete, but I become the best version of myself – in mind, body and spirit. I run four days a week and am on track for the New York marathon in 2022. I have learnt to love and care for myself because I matter too.

Running takes me to my Zen. It has strengthened my body and mind and taught me that I can achieve the incredible. I run for fitness, health, fun, achievement, the honour of Maddi and the massacred ponies. I run for me.

What have I gained from this journey thus far?

The knowledge that forgiveness is vital. In forgiving those who do awful things, you free yourself from being bound to them energetically and, instead, you can harness your energy to achieve great things. I founded a horse sanctuary that stands against abuse in any form. I also model to schoolchildren that anyone can make a positive difference in the world. All you need is a kind intention.

My experience has also taught me that we can always choose how we respond to trauma. We can let it devour us, or we can channel it into positive movement and outcomes.

'Resilience' is a fantastic word to use. To me, it conjures up an image of a tough Amazon woman with armour, yet soft underneath. Resilience is about finding your inner warrior and calling on your inner strengths to guide you through your own healing, and then the healing of others.

For anyone stuck in pain, reach out. This is so important. Reach out to someone you trust, someone who can be your anchor. I was lucky to have all my animals to ground me and support me. Recording your journey can also be helpful. If you look at journal entries during or after trauma, you may be surprised how much you change over time.

I now live with peace, joy and am no longer in fear of speaking my truth. I buy colourful running clothes and feel excited about the marathon, and my life! I am reversing ageing! The weight is peeling off, and I look in the mirror and see bright, glistening eyes looking back at me. I am a warrior woman, and you can find your inner warrior too.

Chapter 21

Back in the Saddle

Jamie Ryder

Rising from a broken back and bankruptcy.

'Character is the only thing that matters, and tragedies give you opportunities to evolve your character.'

Raised by a strong-minded and dominant father and a loving and empathetic mother, I was a very respectful, yet highly spirited country boy. I had a happy childhood in an earthy environment where martial arts and horses were a big feature, as was middle-distance running.

When I was four and a half years old, I won an 'under sevens' race, which spurred my competitive drive. From that day on, I sprung out of bed at a quarter to six and trained everyday – rain, hail or shine. My father drilled self-discipline into me – there was no such thing as a sick day or excuses. The rewards for my effort paid off with records to this day that haven't been beaten and walls of ribbons and shelves of shiny trophies. It was years later, however, that I learned that these accolades were not the true reward.

Although successful on the running track, I was a low achiever at school. Having dyslexia, I barely scraped through most subjects, yet I was highly gifted in maths. When a new mathematics concept was introduced, I could immediately see the logic in it and averaged 98 percent. Unfortunately, my school wasn't interested in nurturing that strength. Instead, I was told to leave and do an apprenticeship – 'Get a job, or we'll expel you.'

I was already familiar with work as I had started my first business at the age of nine, when I ran my neighbour's whippets for $1 each, five days per week. By 12, I had started a window and car cleaning business where I would ride my bike from property to property with buckets and sponges in hand. By 14, I had a part time job detailing cars. I later stepped into the world of horses and became a farrier apprentice. The day I became qualified, I started yet another business and became one of the most respected farriers in my area. To work and income opportunities, I always said 'yes'!

At the of age 21, I had the sole custody of my beautiful daughter and, with this new responsibility, I needed to lift my game.

I shod, trained, traded and rode horses from before the sun rose to after it had set. With the drive to provide for my daughter, my never say never, nothing is impossible attitude, teamed with my ego and need for affirmation, I soon became known as the man/idiot who could shoe horses no one else could shoe and ride horses no one could ride.

I recall riding a thoroughbred one day, bareback and bridle-less. Startled by a strike of lightning, he took off, skidded into a gate, and catapulted me into the air. I landed on the ground with a back-breaking snap. But, I had responsibilities and kept driving forward. I had been trained to ignore pain, to see admission of pain as weakness and to never give up, so this is what I did right up into the day I collapsed. My body simply couldn't continue, and my internal system was shutting down from the overuse of pain medication and excessive alcohol consumption to mask the pain.

At 25, my farrier career was over, my business and hobbies were gone. I was broken, immobilised, and grieving, although at the time, I did not admit it.

So, while laying on my back unable to move, I thought about my responsibility to my daughter. There was no way I was going to let her down. I needed to reinvent myself quickly. Focusing on my losses and limitations didn't occur to me. Instead, I focused on what I *could* do!

I got myself upright, started walking again, bought a cheap suit and applied for a job with a large financial planning company. I mean I was great at maths right! They sent me to one of Australia's most respected business leaders in global human resources and recruitment for a psychological evaluation. Not only did I epically fail this evaluation, but I was told that I had 'no ability to learn' and that I shouldn't be employed.

However, I refused to let the opinion of another person define my career. Instead, I offered to work for six months voluntarily, to pay my own way, to back myself and harness my strengths and work on my weaknesses. I got the job and became the top salesperson within six months and sales manager within 12 months. My rise in the corporate world had begun.

I mastered my trade, sharpened my skills and for nearly two decades, I managed, built up, bought, and sold many multi-million-dollar companies. I built a lot of wealth for many people. I would deliver every time and learned the valuable lesson that if it 'ain't written, it ain't real.' Old school country values didn't live in the corporate world, and I was screwed over many times. Each time I rose again and again. When I was 44, I was running my own business with over 70 employees and was screwed over again and forced into bankruptcy. My family and I lost *everything*, and my self-worth was smashed.

When sleeping, I would have recurring dreams of suicide. I would wake, dripping from head to toe in sweat and literally shake my head to clear these thoughts because awake, such thoughts did not exist. I would lay back down, start to doze and immediately be back in the nightmare.

During this time, I created my own false reality. I saw my loss as me being a loser. I saw my failure as me being a failure, and that loss and failure defined me.

How wrong was I!

Yes, I was the common denominator. Yes, I made mistakes. Yes, it was my responsibility and ultimately, yes it was my fault. With the help of a mentor and my incredible resilient wife, I found the power in 100% responsibility. I found the power in vulnerability, and I found myself through this tragedy. I won through loss and succeeded though failure. I gained perception, value, depth, meaning, experience, character, and humility. And through this, I found my purpose.

How did I morph my self-destructive belief systems and mindset? I shifted my perspective. I wrote a list of 100 things that were good about my bankruptcy. My mentor and I came up with the term 'Slaying the Bankruptcy Dragon', which really resonated with my fighting spirit.

This list was the start of a massive perspective shift and included things like:

- I lost nothing of true value.

- The application of gratitude in adversity is how you find the lessons, wisdom, knowledge and experience life is gifting you.

- The foundation of self-worth is self-trust.

- Discernment is a key element of loyalty and commitment.

- Acceptance, detachment, and clarity are key to good decision making.

- It is critical to take time to listen to and trust in your intuition.

- In life we must have integrity for ourselves in the same way we do our loved ones.

- You either win or you learn.
- Accepting vulnerability is strength.
- Time is our most valuable asset and therefore success is measured in quality time spent, not financial dollars accumulated.
- Self-discovery is an opportunity for personal development.
- To live in the present and detach from both the past (a time that no longer exists) and the future (a time that does not yet exist).
- Bad things can be great things in disguise.
- The only thing that can break me, is me.

From this fresh perspective, I decided that:

- If I act on my dreams, I will succeed.
- If I surround myself with good people, I will succeed.
- If I accept help, I will succeed.
- If I am passionate about what I do, I will succeed.
- If I focus on adding value, I will succeed.
- If I stay humble, others will succeed.

With this new perspective on life, I set off to rebuild myself again and went back into running businesses for other people. Although I was successful, I was not fulfilled. I started posting videos on TikTok to share some of my life's learnings, in the hope that I could help or potentially save just one lost soul. Almost overnight I had over 400,000 followers. I now work in 15 countries around the world, helping people overcome trauma, rebuild their self-worth and to live their lives with freedom, fulfilment, and gratitude.

Today, I am working 100% with purpose and have found my place in this world. I believe that life doesn't happen *to* you, rather life happens *for* you. Therefore, if we learn the art of controlling the direction of our thoughts, we all have the power to change our lives.

Life is not a lineal journey, and each one of us have travelled a unique path to get to this very day. But here's the kicker. It's the story you tell yourself today, which is based on your beliefs, that will affect you tomorrow.

I challenge and empower people to shift their belief systems, to be aware of what is and is not serving them; to learn how to set, manage and maintain their boundaries and to speak their truth with peaceful confidence so they can trust themselves again. This self-trust will start rebuilding self-respect which builds self-worth, and here is where lives can change.

The accolades I won as a young athlete weren't the true prize. It was the character I developed in training that was the true reward and it is this character that defines me. My top seven-character traits are resilience, truthfulness, trustworthiness, courage, wisdom, empathy and discernment. Once you understand the character that resides within you, you will start seeing your self-worth. Character is the only thing that matters, and tragedies give you opportunities to evolve your character.

Know that you are not alone. We all need authentic and genuine conversations. Asking for help and connection is not a weakness. In fact, it's a sign of enormous courage and strength. Resilience is vital because the ability to get back in the saddle is critical.

Never give up. Never quit. Stay strong.

Chapter 22

A Life of Passion and Purpose

Steve Parish OAM

How a lifelong passion for inspiring others to connect to nature provided strength when life's challenges seemed insurmountable.

'The void the loss created was essential to empowering new growth in my professional and personal life. It opened new, previously unimagined doors.'

I was raised in Adelaide in the 1950s under very strict parentage. My father struggled his whole life to express his feelings, and my mother found solace in Apostolic Pentecostalism – a cult that resisted all radio and television and heavily restricted what books were allowed in the house. Fortunately, *National Geographic* was allowed. Regulations aside, my mother practised faith-healing and exorcisms in her study next to my bedroom sleep out. As a boy, I was terrified.

Seen through the prism of time, I was in my 60s before I could forgive my mother for what I consider was childhood spiritual abuse. Unfortunately, we never had a conversation that healed the lifelong rift between us. Mother firmly believed that whatever path I travelled, I would never find happiness outside of total devotion to God-based teachings defined by the protocols of her chosen cult. The parentage I received severely affected my formal education and, in turn, my self-esteem.

Throughout my life, I've had my share of life challenges. Let's face it, who hasn't! Looking back, I now see that throughout life, I have suffered from what I now see as a relentless obsession with 'poor little me' mind stories, all related to a childhood erosion of self-belief.

As a boy, I collected firearms. In fact, I was so obsessed with guns that I even started an apprenticeship as a gunsmith! Armed to the teeth, I would sit in my bedroom with a gun barrel in my mouth, contemplating ending 'it' all. These thoughts haunted me for decades. I now believe that my lifetime struggles with anxiety and depression led directly to cancer and heart disease.

While issues with relationships and health should have been enough to force change in my life, it was not until the loss of my life's work, embodied in a multi-million-dollar publishing and photography company, that I finally began to 'wake up' to the fact that so much of my anxiety and depression was directly attached to what I now refer to as 'mind stories'.

In 2011, Brisbane's riverside properties and structures associated with flood plain channels were severely flooded. Our publishing studio and warehouse were situated next to a major waterway. Unfortunately, insurance would not come to the party due to a single clause. The policy covered flood and not 'inundation'! While struggling to rebuild severely damaged stock holdings, we were also hit with the loss of revenue due to a significant downturn in the retail stores we supplied. At the time, the company had an annual turnover of over $15 million. After struggling for 12 months, we appointed receivers and proceeded into voluntary bankruptcy.

After handing over the keys to our company and home and having my life's work placed in an ad for sale, I began a significant personal awakening, albeit in between some major anxiety attacks, several of which saw me admitted to hospital. While the term 'spiritual teacher' initially caused a negative reaction from childhood experiences, I started listening to globally renowned spiritual teacher Eckhardt Tolle's *The Power of Now* CDs and one in particular, 'Facing Adversity', hit home, especially this single quote.

*'You can only lose something that you have,
but you cannot lose something that you are.'*

Eckhart Tolle

Through Eckhart Tolle's teachings, I began to appreciate that my wellbeing was influenced by constantly replaying my 'poor little me' mind stories, which included: *I had no formal education. My mother didn't love me,* and so on. And so, with nothing other than a laptop and my digital image library (purchased by a publisher who invested in my bankrupted company's assets), I began to develop an online Masterclass: 'PHOTOGRAPHY: A Pathway to Purpose'.

We can flip our mind story in an instant, anytime, anywhere. It's a matter of being aware of the stories we tell ourselves. In 1995, I walked into a medical diagnosis session with my doctor with all the woes of the world on my shoulder. My burgeoning business was a source of both excitement and fear. After a series of x-rays, I was informed I had a large tumour. In a flash, what was so important 60 seconds earlier had evaporated, and my life suddenly had a new focus – survival. After surgery, I noticed how blue the sky was, how green and full of life the trees had become. I was literally shaken awake and catapulted into the present moment.

As I look back over the past 26 years, I realise that while a significant event can jolt you into the present moment, one can easily back-slide unless investment is made to inner engineering.

Wild creatures face challenges every day. What sets them apart from humans is that they don't indulge in 'poor little me' stories about life's hardships. When two Tasmanian devils battle over food, or two male kangaroos fight for mating rights, they don't let losing become a resentful mind story that defeats them for decades to come.

I began to realise that my anxieties were primarily based on my specific mind stories that focused on me being a victim, and that all I had to do was acknowledge that these were unhelpful, then draw the curtains to close yet another stage performance.

I further awoke to the fact that two of me were performing the story – one was replaying the story, and the other was the witnessing presence, the observer of the story. After the floods and bankruptcy, Eckhart Tolle's teachings helped me to refocus. The void the loss created was essential to empowering new growth in my professional and personal life. It opened new, previously unimagined doors. It certainly didn't mean there was no pain – there was plenty, and at times it was magnified by my over-active imagination!

Dealing with loss is a choice, and a tenacious spirit can endure and transform loss if we choose to let it. Having a Creative Life Purpose (CLP) certainly helps. Passion and purpose are mortal enemies of anxiety and depression. Auguste Rodin wrote, 'Love your calling with passion, it is the meaning of your life.' Your CLP can be a lighthouse beacon bringing wealth, in all its forms, into your life. When you're passionate and purposeful, you create blessings for yourself and all those you encounter.

My CLP has guided me through very challenging times. It has allowed me to see, feel and act, on pivotal opportunities, to steer me in the right direction, rather than feeling lost and worrying about the past and possible events. Understanding and communicating our purpose within the world is one of the most important things we can ever do.

Alone in the wilderness of the Kimberley in 1984, I found my CLP by following my heart. When we listen carefully when our heart is giving direction, decisions can be made in harmony with who we truly are. My CLP is to inspire others to regard the natural world as essential to spiritual, mental and physical wellbeing.

For humans to care for habitats, we must first appreciate that we are intrinsically part of the environment, and our life is enhanced by appreciating and caring for nature. A CLP is not about your ego. It's about giving, connecting, inspiring, making a difference. Define your Creative Life Purpose, embrace it and do the work. Work hard because you love to work hard, not because you want a reward. Our CLP should not be separate from our everyday life situations. Our real-life purpose can only be achieved when body, mind and spirit are in harmony.

Adversity is part of being human. Your experience of loss can mean it's time for a fresh start, especially if your Creative Life Purpose has already been established before your life-changing loss. Do not underestimate the power of a CLP, especially when it is connected to something as powerful as the natural world and the broader community with whom you share your life.

When the economy falters or a pandemic strikes, the media adds to the collective distress of the general population. However, if we reject the collective anxiety (by not watching the news over and over, or not contributing to social upheaval on social media), our lives remain much more positive, and we can focus more on the joy that our Creative Life Purpose brings us.

Most importantly, never give up!

I once watched a wombat stand and stare at a huge wire-mesh fence. The fence seemed impenetrable even to me, and no doubt it did to the wombat too! Nonetheless, the wombat stood and eyeballed it for what seemed like ages. Then, lowering his head, he charged, hitting the bottom of the fence at full wombat speed. The wall of wire lifted, and through the creature went. A few metres past it, he stopped, turned and stared at the fence again. Then, as though having congratulated itself, the wombat turned around and vanished into a thicket. Such tenacity! He didn't just imagine it. He did it! Then again, those who know wombats know their determination. When hell-bent on a path to travel, they don't give up. Maybe there are many life lessons we can learn from wombats.

Chapter 23
Not on My Watch

Chad Staples

Rising from bushfires that ravaged our zoo.

*'When you feel confident,
you feel competent and trust that you
can cope with whatever happens.
When you feel confident, people
around you feel the same.'*

As a young boy, I knew I would grow up and work with animals. I've been lucky in that nothing has bumped me off that trajectory. From a junior zookeeper to Managing Director of Australian Wildlife Parks, I've been blessed with a 25-year career with animals.

My home is in the heart of the 65-acre Mogo Wildlife Park, on the New South Wales south coast, along with 200 animals – gorillas, ostriches, lions, tamarins, pandas, zebras, giraffes, meerkats, tigers, gibbons, otters, chimpanzees, orangutans, snow leopards and reptiles. When I hear the lions roaring and the gibbons singing each night, I know that all is well and sleep soundly. My wellbeing is inextricably linked to the wellbeing of every animal in my care.

In December 2019, the south coast was ablaze with bushfires. Smoke had been filling our air for months. We knew we were in danger and prepared for the worst. Armed with vast reservoirs of recycled water, water tanks on the back of utes, fire extinguishers, buckets and wet hessian sacks, our sole objective was to keep the animals and ourselves safe.

Each day, the situation became increasingly perilous as the smoke thickened and the fires raced towards us from all directions.

At 6 am on New Year's Eve, the sky had an ominous red tinge, and the community of Mogo was told to evacuate to the beach. Not on my watch. Just as a parent who wouldn't leave their children to perish, I would not leave our animals. Nor would 12 other staff members who ignored the authority's orders that day.

So began the fight. The fight for our lives and the lives of our animal family.

We began by watering the perimeter with 200,000 litres of water. Then we moved the big animals – seven lions, two orangutans and four gorillas – into their night dens where they sleep. With water and bountiful supplies of their favourite treats, they went in without hesitation.

The giraffes were understandably nervous as we ushered them into a large yard, which had been fireproofed. With their strong herd instinct, they stuck together and had each other's backs. Throughout the entire ordeal, we kept talking to them, calmly, reminding them that they were in good hands.

The keepers packed up the small animals most at risk, including the red pandas and primates, in individual containers and put them in my house for safety.

The fires were upon us, and the fight was intense. Although it was daytime, the sky was black. It felt like Armageddon, a cataclysmic struggle against overwhelming forces. The fire was not only attacking us from the ground, but it was also reaching over us, dropping firebombs the size of cars. None of us had ever been trained or fought bushfires before, but we were united with our uncompromised focus to defend, defend, defend.

I called 000 twice to ask for help, but the resources were depleted, and no help came. In the afternoon, the wind changed, which subverted our fighting strategy. Chaos reigned into the night.

At 10 pm, we finally had reprieve and knew we had won.

Night patrols and the extinguishing of spot fires continued for another five days. Although nearly 80 percent of the property was burned, including the entire boundary fence, not a single animal was harmed.

The focus then switched from survival to recovery. Not only my personal recovery, but the recovery of our park, our dedicated staff, and our community. Mogo was a community in crisis.

We had no power for days afterwards, which created problems for food storage, for both human and animal food. At least 20 people arrived at the park seeking refuge, some with their own animals. Media from all over the world suddenly arrived. Food trucks arrived. It was unprecedented mayhem, and I felt responsible for everyone involved, including, of course, the animals. This state of hyper-vigilance and stress lasted for at least six weeks after the fires.

Like all tough experiences, my healing from this experience can be attributed to not one singular factor, but many factors. Succeeding to save all our animals gave me a good first step to recovery, though, at the same time, I was devastated by the millions of other animals in the fires who didn't survive, and the many people left homeless and in trauma. For months afterwards, my emotions oscillated between euphoria and grief, and everywhere in between.

Being with our animals, however, was hugely restorative for me. During my quiet times with them, I noticed how quickly they adjusted to life after the fires. They knew they were safe. They knew the trauma was over. They were in the present moment, which made it easier for me to 'just be'.

On 23 December, a week before the fires, a lion cub was born at the park. Phoenix, as he was named, not only brought joy to me, the staff and the wider Mogo community, he became the symbol of hope and rejuvenation for people across Australia and the world. We were flooded with messages from well-wishers and people whose spirits lifted from the birth of

Phoenix. I was amazed by the love and support we received and learnt from this how deeply we are all connected, humans and animals, in both suffering and joy.

This was one of many lessons I learnt from the bushfires. In fact, I learnt more from the bushfires and the aftermath, than I could in any courses or books, particularly in relation to leadership. The experience affirmed to me the importance of leading by example: empathy with everyone around you; the power of words, particularly words of praise; being supportive; and being confident during crisis.

If you were flying through a rough storm in an aeroplane, the last thing passengers and crew need is a nervous pilot. When you feel confident, you feel competent and trust that you can cope with whatever happens. When you feel confident, people around you feel the same, and this is essential in emergencies.

These lessons are gifts from the bushfires, which I will always be grateful for.

Two years on and my life is busy, productive and fulfilling. I continue to live on the premises of the park, which I love. Knowing that a healthy body contributes to a healthy mind, I eat nutritious food, and for one hour every day, I work out in my home gym near the lions. I often watch them looking at me, and I wonder what they're thinking! Working out releases endorphins and always makes me feel better. Healthy lifestyle habits undoubtedly help resilience and wellbeing.

With deep gratitude, the animals in the park are well and multiplying. Phoenix, who is one of our most popular animals, is now two years old and living with a new lioness. One of our greatest achievements since the fires is the construction of a new veterinary hospital to help the park's animals and rescued wildlife. By having a passion for animals that is fulfilled through my work and home environment, I'm in a good place.

I'm aware that, in the future, certain things – such as smoke, summer heat and dryness – could trigger fear associated with the bushfires. However, I believe that a major part of resilience is being prepared for hard times. Just as we prepared ourselves for the fire, we can prepare ourselves for hard times. By anticipating triggers, I'll be ready to calm my mind. If stress occurs, I'll remind myself that – we're safe now. It's over.

My advice to people who are struggling from trauma is to be honest with yourself about where you're at. If you're not ok, talk to a professional person to help you. Keep looking until you find someone you're comfortable with. Healing takes effort, not just time. So, work on your mental health as you'd work on your physical health. Seeking help when you're vulnerable is not a weakness. It shows mental and emotional awareness and strength to lean on others, just as you'd want others to lean on you when they need to.

Chapter 24

A Voice for the Voiceless

Sara Tilling

Rising from the ashes after a catastrophic bushfire.

'As the animals heal and grow, so do we.'

Imagine their terror when the fires encircled them, leaving them nowhere to run. Imagine their pain as they're bodies melted away. Such thoughts continue to haunt me, and if I pretend that I've recovered from the New Year's Eve bushfires of 2019, I'm not being honest. It's still raw, very raw, and I'm not the same person I was before. However, the fires were a monumental test of my character and, for the animals, I'm not giving up.

My partner Gary and I have been wildlife carers for ten years, initially for birds, then fate sent macropods (wallabies and kangaroos) our way. Driving along a road one day, a joey fell out of her mother's pouch. We pulled over and sat with the joey for an hour, hoping her mother would return. She didn't return and our irreversible love affair with macropods began.

Once you get to know macropods, I mean *really* get to know their individual personalities, there's no turning back! Female kangaroos who we have rescued, rehabilitated and released, would come back to us to proudly show us their joeys. Moments like that fuel my soul so deeply that I know unequivocally that my life purpose is to help eastern kangaroos.

In 2018, we decided to move from Port Macquarie and settle on the south coast of New South Wales. We moved to an 850-acre property near Cobargo, which was a haven for 300–400 kangaroos, wallabies, wombats and birds. We also had our pet goats and a handful of rescued rabbits.

When the fire struck, Gary and I were in Tasmania. We had a caretaker on the property to protect the animals. The first fire was two kilometres from the property and went past. Shortly afterwards, it created its own 'tornado system' and turned back on the property in three directions. The caretaker left and almost all the animals died.

On 1 January (the next day), we came home. People told us to prepare ourselves. 'It was a war zone,' they said.

And how true that was.

No buildings were left. Animal bodies were strewn across the burnt paddocks; the bodies of the poor animals who couldn't outrun it. When we heard a noise under some tin where our house stood the day before, we approached and immediately smelt burnt skin and flesh. It was a wallaby. Blood seeped out of her eyes, ears and nose. How could she still be alive, I wondered. All we had was an axe and some sedation. With a hard blow to her head, she was gone. I sat and looked around at the smouldering ground, a surreal lifeless ground, and sobbed. And it wasn't a 'everything will be ok tomorrow' sob, but a soulful, 'feeling the horror of the animals' sob.

There were no favourites. I loved them all. Danny was a rescued 'roo who I cared for since he was a sickly three kilograms. I nursed him to health for six weeks, and he would come to me from afar when I stood on the top of the hill and sang out to him, 'Danny, Dan, Dan ...' He'd always come for a cuddle. Just before the fire came, the caretaker said that Danny came and looked at him, asking him for help. He was never seen again. I struggle with the extreme guilt of not being there for our Danny Dan Dan ... and the other animals. We would have saved at least some of them.

Gabbi, a kangaroo, came back after the fire, but the entire front of her body had melted off. We sedated and euthanised her. Another wallaby came up to us for help. We gave him pain relief and antibiotics and let him go. At that stage, we had no facilities to contain the injured animals. We had no facilities to sleep in ourselves. Molly was 'my girl'. She miraculously appeared, jumped around in circles then disappeared, never seen again.

Two months later, my father passed away in New Zealand. It was the start of COVID, and I couldn't travel to New Zealand to be with him. The stack of stressors kept building, relentlessly. There were moments when I considered giving up and there were moments when Gary considered giving up. Fortunately, those moments didn't coincide. We pulled each other out of our black holes, and I'm forever grateful to Gary for being there. Sometimes stress or trauma divides couples, but in our case, it strengthened our bond. It's unbreakable.

Although tested, our commitment to the conservation of eastern kangaroos is also unbreakable, and I realise that this sense of purpose has given us strength to rebuild our sanctuary and our lives. As we watch the animals heal and grow, so do we. Nature is my best therapy. It grounds me, restores my energy and nourishes my soul. Gary and I are extremely busy with our full-time jobs (which pay our bills) and full-time care of the animals. Some of them require 24 hours of attention. But whenever we get an opportunity to be home together, we sit on the hill and just be. The animals always join us, and a sense of joy, privilege and gratitude overcomes me. Such moments are enough reward to sustain and strengthen me.

I think society would benefit from these experiences. If more people had a stronger connection with animals and nature and less on materialism and technology, we'd have a better world, a kinder and more sustainable world.

Gratitude plays a big role in my recovery. Not only am I grateful for Gary and the animals, but I am also blessed with so many people who have supported us through this ordeal. Kipa Anne, for example, relocated seven joeys to us to care for after the fires and provided unwavering support. The joeys confirmed and affirmed our life purpose, and Kipa has become an incredible friend. My dear friend Nikki created a fundraising page to help us rebuild. Our friend Scott helped Gary to rebuild some enclosures so we could continue caring for animals. And a lady came all the way from Sydney to give us a dryer to help us clean the animals' bedding. A fellow macropod carer, Lucille, messaged me every day for over a year, just to let us know that we were surrounded by love and support. Our local vet, Carl von Schreiber, has also been compassionate and helpful. I will never forget the kindness and generosity of our friends, Heather and Cheryl, who purchased a caravan for us to live in when we were numb and shell-shocked.

Animals Australia, Animal Rescue Cooperative and the Creative Cowboys film company have all been a wonderful support and have given the wildlife a voice. I'm also thankful to the other volunteers who helped us with daily feed drops of fresh fruit and vegetables for the animals. My mother has also been a source of strength, despite dealing with her own grief. Every act of support and kindness will be remembered for the rest of my life.

When you see people suffering through a hard time, never underestimate the value of an act of kindness. Even small acts of kindness, bestowed at the right time, can make a big difference to their recovery. Don't be frightened to offer help, or to be helped. We all need it sometime.

A little while after the bushfires, I looked for any gifts that might come from this tragedy. About a *billion* Australian animals were killed. Perhaps their loss would wake people up to the importance of their conservation and welfare. You might remember that there was a lot of public concern … for a moment. But then suddenly COVID struck and swamped the voice of wildlife. Only months later, despite the catastrophic losses, did the Victorian and New South Wales governments resume the dispensing of kangaroo 'harvesting' permits. Forget the animals! It's back to business as usual! To me, this is the greatest tragedy of the fires.

Gary and I now live in a shipping container on the property and have rescued some 150 animals, with over 40 being successfully rehabilitated and released in the last 15 months – mostly victims of road hits. Our mission, to provide a safe place for them to live and educate the public about compassion and respect to *all* animals, is stronger than ever. To achieve this, I work full time to pay the bills and Gary runs the sanctuary full time.

All they want to do is live in their mob, yet they are the most persecuted land mammal in the world. Not many people know that when a kangaroo is 'harvested' (shot), their joey's head is smashed on the ground or against a tree to kill them. Imagine the public outrage if it was legal to kill dogs this way. It's not acceptable to hit a dog on the road and drive on, yet it's common for people to hit kangaroos on the road, curse them and leave them to die slowly in pain. Most of our rescued kangaroos are from motor vehicle accidents. Whether you're a dog or a kangaroo, their suffering is equal. This is my passion and purpose that drives me to get up and work every day.

My advice to other people who are trying to heal from bushfire trauma, is to adopt a 'tested, but never beaten' attitude. Be a survivor, not a victim. Sometimes, you may need to force yourself to get up and keep going. That's when you need self-discipline. No matter how dark the hole is in your mind, there is always a light. Have faith that the light will get brighter. That's optimism. If you find a purpose to make the world a little better, you will feel better too.

Chapter 25

Light Bulb Moments

Mark Tregellas

Rising from police-work trauma.

'There is not a police officer with over 20 years of operational experience who is not angry and does not suffer PTSI to a greater or lesser extent.'

As an explorer, commando and police officer, my life has been a rich adventure. After growing up in Melbourne and finishing high school, I worked and saved for a year, then left Australia for the adventure of a lifetime. Four years and 52 countries later, I came home. With more than a lifetime's worth of experiences, which included kayaking up the Amazon, climbing in the Himalayas and travelling with ivory poachers and gun runners in Ethiopia, I felt I needed a career that would match. So, I joined the 1st Commando Regiment. After four years, I decided to become a police officer, which is what I did for the next 31 years.

During my police career, the majority of which was working by myself in remote rural areas, I was shot, broke my back, knee, shoulder, elbow and was twice diagnosed with post-traumatic stress disorder (PTSD). I have never liked the term PTSD. Disorder implies a disability, disadvantage or distress. PTSD is an injury to a person's brain as the result of being exposed to single or multiple critical incidents either directly or vicariously. I prefer to call it post-traumatic stress injury (PTSI).

There are generally two types of PTSI.

The first is the result of exposure to a single incident, such as a vehicle collision or a bank robbery. The other is exposure to multiple incidents over time, and this mainly affects military and first responders. Soldiers, police, ambulance, rescue, and fire services personnel are usually resistant to the first type. You wouldn't be in that type of job if you weren't.

One incident I still dream about involves a 150-kilogram male who had a psychotic episode. He had tried to strangle himself with a dog's collar in front of me after telling me he intended to kill himself. When I went to clear the back of the police car, I turned around and saw he had grabbed a jerry can of petrol from the back of his boat, poured it over himself and was walking towards the fire carrying the can. I sprinted over and grabbed him a pace away. It was then I found out he was stronger than me.

We struggled and petrol slopped and dribbled down the can almost to the fire. I was fully expecting it to explode, and we would both be burnt. At that moment, he dropped the can. The world went into slow motion. The can hit the ground, staying bolt upright. I breathed a sigh of relief until the man reached over, grabbed me with both hands and tried to pull me into the fire with him. All semblance of professionalism went out the door. He was screaming. I was screaming. I had images of my youngest daughter flashing through my mind. Suddenly, he slipped, and I twisted his arm, pulling him away from the fire. I handcuffed him and lay on the ground getting my breath back. It was over.

I was honoured to receive a bravery award for saving his life, and at the time I was asked why I did it. My answer was this: 'When you become a police officer, you take an oath. That oath binds you to act when called upon or when circumstances demand such action. The decision to act is easy. The question you ask yourself is what would I do if it were my loved ones in danger? How would I want others to act?'

For many years, I was able to deal with critical incidents. Fatal collisions, domestic violence, assaults, cot deaths, child neglect and abuse, rape and murder are all part of a police officer's life. But everyone has their limit. After 31 years and one month as a police officer and suffering a second diagnosis of PTSI, I retired on a medical pension.

I was able to deal with critical incidents during my career in part due to my schema. Your schema is the mental structure that an individual uses to organise knowledge and guide cognitive processes and behaviour. It's kind of like the moral framework you use to interpret and predict the world. Police and military have similar schema that share three characteristics: self-sacrificing, unrelenting standards, and they tend to see things in black and white.

It's seeing things only in black and white that causes problems, because most people see things in shades of grey. If a police officer knows a person has a previous conviction for a serious offence, they will always see that person in that context, even if they have shown remorse, been to court, served a period of prison and are reformed. Police do not forgive easily. Most other people though are willing to forgive and forget. This process though tends to make you angry.

PTSI and anger are intimately linked. If you can lower your anger, you lower your PTSI by a significant amount. For police officers dealing with offenders that have committed serious violent crimes, your anger towards them increases over the years because they see the courts deliver penalties that seem too light and then the perpetrator is released to re-offend. I doubt there is not a police officer with over 20 years of operational experience who is not angry and does not suffer PTSI to a greater or lesser extent. So, lowering your anger will lower your PTSI – but how do you do this?

I was taught three ways:

- When you feel yourself getting angry, ask yourself why you are so angry. Is your anger out of proportion to the situation at hand?

- Try and see it from the other person's perspective.

- Lastly, in the greater scheme of life, does it really matter?

It was the third one that made the most sense to me. This technique worked well for everyday interactions but not for the major incidents that had affected me.

On a recent trip to East Timor, I met 'Green Leaf', a freedom fighter who had been tortured by the Indonesians to the point of leaving him with permanent physical disabilities. Walking through the prison where he was once incarcerated, he talked in vivid detail about what had been done to him. It was harrowing. At the end, I asked him if he was angry at the Indonesians for what they had done. He smiled and said, 'No, not at all, I have forgiven.' Confused, I asked him how he could forgive them. He then explained that he did not forgive the Indonesians, he had forgiven himself for letting his experience and anger go, so he could have a life.

This was a light bulb moment for me. I had been looking at forgiveness the wrong way. This knowledge made me rethink my life and all the things that had happened in it. Changing the way I thought about forgiveness started to lower my anger and in turn my PTSI.

I could now sleep better, get angry much less and start to look at other methods to help even more. Chief among them was meditation. I had never been able to meditate. Clearing your mind, staying in the present, being mindful were concepts I could not grasp. Then I tried the Wim Hof Method – take 40 deep breaths, exhaling each time unforced, and then stop breathing for as long as you can, which forces you to relax. Your mind clears because you are concentrating on not breathing. It was another light bulb moment. When I started, I could not hold my breath for a minute. My record is now three minutes 40 seconds.

I combined this with cold inoculation. You start off gradually by taking tepid and then increasingly cold showers and then progress to ice baths. Years of military and police work meant I had the discipline to do this – but what I was not expecting was the total relaxation and meditative state it produced. Immersing yourself in freezing water for five minutes sounds crazy, but you not only get used to it, you look forward to it, and the chemical reactions that occur in your body are beneficial. I have not had a cold since taking ice baths. It's not for everyone, but it worked for me.

Everyone's journey with PTSI is different. What worked for me might not work for someone else. What I hope is that my story might provide a light bulb moment for someone reading it so they can start their journey to recovery.

Chapter 25

Chapter 26
Second Chance

Adam Smith

**Rising from depression, attempted suicide
and my subsequent disabilities.**

*'Although I'm forced to walk the earth in darkness,
I can now see light in all areas of my life.'*

Footy, pies, beers, mates, girlfriend, car, my own house. What more could a young man want?

Mental health, as it turns out.

In 2004, I was struggling with depression, despite everything in my life going so well. There is nothing I can point to for causing it. I had a happy childhood in a country town with two great parents. I worked for my father as a painter and decorator, felt a part of my community and was the Captain and Best and Fairest Player for my footy team.

However, I didn't talk to anyone about how I was feeling. There was stigma around mental illness back then. Instead, I planned to end the pain through suicide. It was just a matter of when and how.

I had an old rifle that was stored in pieces. One day, I sat down and assembled the pieces together, ready for the 'right' time.

In my typical way, I had a party at my place on a Saturday night. There was lots of booze and drugs. My girlfriend and I had an argument, and she left the party. Drunk, high and angry, I grabbed my gun and stormed out to my car. One of my mates tried to stop me, but I drove off, almost knocking him over as I fled.

Minutes later, I crashed into a tree, but that didn't stop me. The engine still worked, so on I drove to a clearing. I parked the car, sat in the passenger seat, pointed the rifle to my temple, then *bang*. I pulled the trigger.

Unbeknown to me, a woman was assaulted in the same place the day before. Early Sunday morning, she brought police officers to the area to show them where the assault took place. Suddenly, the police had a whole new case to deal with.

Chapter 26

Miraculously, they found me alive six hours after I shot myself. Emergency surgery at the Albury Hospital kept me alive, then I was flown to Melbourne for four months of complex surgeries and rehabilitation. While the incredible skills of the surgeons were able to keep me alive, I lost my senses of smell and sight.

Hospital was like a twilight zone. It wasn't my past, nor my future. It was black, painful, frightening yet safe place, somewhere in between. I remember the day I walked out of hospital and moved into my mother's place. I was of course grateful for my mother, but also nervous. It was my first day of my new life – my second chance at life.

I was sad about not being able to stay in my own house, sad that I lost my vision and smell and sad that I blew away everything I had. Most of all, I was sad about all the heartache I caused to so many people.

I thought about my good mate who tried to stop me. The angst I put him through. I thought about the woman and police officers who found my blasted, bleeding body. I'm sure it's a vision that will haunt them forever. I thought about my mates and family who really love me. They expected me to die and were planning my funeral.

I'm not going to pretend that my recovery was easy. It wasn't. I had to learn how to adapt to a world without light. At first, simple things like dressing myself were a struggle. It was a slow but sure road to recovery.

My football club generously raised funds for me that enabled me to build a unit on Mum's place. This was an important step towards my independence. I was also provided with a guide dog. The first one didn't quite make the grade, but my second dog, Yetta, is awesome. She gives me the freedom to walk to the coffee shop, pub and run my own business.

So, how did I get from that dark hole with a gun at my head, to where I am today?

I got help.

Rather than hiding my pain like I used to, I talk to people I trust – my doctor, counsellor, parents and close mates. I talk *before* it's too late.

I talk to my psychologist every month, and through that, I learn other tools to help me not only stay alive, but to make the best of a bad situation. For example, if I feel that dark hole opening its mouth to grab me, I do something that makes me feel better, such as fishing, having a beer with mates, patting Yetta, or listening to a podcast.

My doctor treats my depression with medication. I've accepted that I'll be on medication for the rest of my life, and that's ok. I promised Mum and Dad that I would never attempt to take my life again, and I honour that commitment, not only for them, but for everyone who loves and cares for me – AND for a higher purpose.

It really is a miracle that I'm alive today, and although I'm not religious, I believe I'm alive for a reason. I'm alive to teach other people who are suffering with depression to not make the same mistake I made. If I can save even one life, my life has meaning.

I'm a lucky man for many reasons. I survived, learnt to appreciate the gift of life, married a wonderful woman, Jan, have two stepchildren, a grandchild, live in a beautiful home in a great community of Albury and run my own business as a massage therapist. Although I'm forced to walk the earth in darkness, I can now see light in all areas of my life.

Jan is my shining star. I can't imagine my life without Jan – my soulmate, wife and carer. At any time, I can tell Jan exactly how I'm feeling without any fear of judgement. Jan is direct with me when she is concerned about my mental health and asks if I need to see my psychologist.

There are times, however, when I feel frustrated. I've never seen my wife. I tend to lose things, and without my sense of smell, I have a low but constant level of worry about fire and smoke.

Nonetheless, my gratitude for what is going well in my life far outweighs my frustrations.

To people who are struggling in that black hole, I say don't take the path I took. There are other, better ways to manage the situation. Firstly, talk to someone. Use your voice. Go to a GP and ask for help. If I talked to a mate or a GP back in 2004 when I assembled my gun, my path would have very different.

When you ask for help, people will come to your aid. You don't need to know all the answers. Don't expect to know all the answers. That's where professional people can help you.

To people who know people who are struggling, I say listen to them. Listen to them without judgement and acknowledge their feelings. Tell them to start by talking to a GP and offer to go with them. Call them that night to check on them. Let them know they're not alone and they're already on the right path by talking.

Talk for your life.

Chapter 27

The Epiphany that Saved Me from Suicide

Mal Missingham

**Rising from depression, alcoholism
and the brink of suicide.**

'I know this is not a temporary recovery phase.

It's permanent.

I've chosen LIFE!'

My story is not exceptional or extraordinary. I'm a mature man who's been a husband, a father, a self-employed, financially secure businessman. I've suffered from depression, alcoholism and have been on the brink of suicide. I'm now living with passionate purpose and can tell you what worked for me.

About 15 years ago, my 'normal' world turned upside down when my wife left me, taking our three teenage children with her. The sun that had normally risen in the east, suddenly rose in the west. I was grief-stricken, lost, disorientated and deeply lonely.

My self-esteem plummeted. I thought I must have been unworthy of my wife, my family. I turned to alcohol to numb my pain. Firstly, in small doses, and then incrementally more and more.

Alcoholism is an insidious addiction. It creeps up in a devious and subtle way. As my dependence on alcohol increased, my work performance and business declined, and the downward journey began. I knew I was on a slippery slide, but my emotional pain, my depression was hard to bear. It was the easiest way to get through each day.

At the time, I also thought I needed to be in a relationship to complete my life. I had a succession of unsuccessful relationships and growing financial pressures. I began selling off some of my belongings to make my mortgage payments, which reinforced my feeling of failure and unworthiness.

COVID then struck, and I had no income, no way out. I didn't want to wake up in the morning. A giant hand was inside my chest crushing me. I had no purpose, no point to continue. Simple tasks, such as having a shower or changing the sheets of my bed, seemed too colossal. With no purpose to get up each morning, I thought, why bother?

One day, I went for a ride on my motorcycle trying to relax. As I rode along, my sub-conscious began scanning for a hard target to ride into. A car or truck was not an option, as I didn't want to harm anyone else. I just wanted the pain to go away. Had I found a concrete wall that day, I wouldn't be here now.

Suicide had become a reality. Then I started thinking about my kids and the effect my suicide would have on them. Initially, I thought they would cope. Then I found an article about parental suicide and the lifelong trauma it can have on children. I realised I didn't want to leave them that legacy. Suicide was no longer my preferred route. While my own pain would end, I'd be causing a lifetime of pain for them – which for me, was not acceptable. My love for my children trumped my desperate desire to escape the pain.

I went to my GP who recommended a free drug and alcohol rehabilitation centre at a public hospital. The intake psychologist there said, 'Would you like last night's drink to be your last?'

It was a surprising, pivotal and 'now, or never' moment. I took a leap of faith and agreed to commit to the program. With the aid of professional counselling, medications and injections of nutritional supplements, the detox stage was made easier. My anxiety was dissolved. I could live with myself again. The rehab program was a critical part of my recovery. It was a central part of a puzzle that I'd been trying, up until then, and failing to put together.

With the love of my children and the wonderful rehab program motivating me, I decided it was time to take responsibility and find other solutions. I realised that I was worth saving. I shifted my attitude of unworthiness to worthiness. Nathaniel's Branden's book – *6 Pillars of Self-Esteem* – helped me to accept myself and, dare I say it, to love myself.

Now I'm a different man. My mojo is back stronger than ever. From my heart, I can say that I've shifted from the brink of suicide to feeling happy, confident, and highly purposeful. My friends are amazed at the change in me. I know this is not a temporary recovery phase. It's permanent. I've chosen LIFE!

There was no singular solution to my current wellbeing. It was like unlocking a combination, solving a puzzle, joining the dots. After years of effort, it all just fell into place.

Once my self-esteem was on the rise, I made more effort to care for myself. I exercise and meditate more regularly. I eat more nutritious food and spend time with close friends, fishing or motorcycling. For the first time, I've lost my need for a partner. For now, that void is filled by my newfound love of myself.

I would not have been able to be where I am today without the support of men's groups. I became involved with Men's Wellbeing, a wonderful community of 'men supporting men'. We meet with vulnerability and honesty and go deep within ourselves. For men, this can be very hard. A lot of us were taught not to be vulnerable, not to cry. Our meetings are nourishing, renewing, and juice for my soul.

There are much better ways to deal with pain than alcohol and suicide. Life will get better if you believe it's possible. For me, it did not matter how miniscule that possibility was. Hang on to the tiniest thread of possibility and reach out for help. The path to a happier life may be closer than imagined and illuminated by the most unexpected sources.

Chapter 27

Chapter 28
The Instinctive Warrior

Jeff Hansen

**Rising from depression to a life of
passion and adventure.**

*'Since living in alignment with my true nature,
my life has been rich and rewarding
beyond my imagination.'*

Growing up in Melbourne, my first love was dinosaurs. As they were no longer around, I switched to reptiles and had many enclosures and even an incubator with baby bearded dragons hatching. I always felt at home in the Australian bush – be that down a creek lifting rocks to see what surprises lay underneath, or up the top of gum trees observing monitor lizards. I always believed that I would grow up to be a wildlife vet, perhaps helping animals in Africa.

For all the wrong reasons, however, I ended up doing a double degree in Electronic Engineering and Computer Science. I travelled the world with this, but looking back now, this choice was slowly eating away at me. I would watch nature documentaries and feel sick to my core, thinking – *how did I get my life so wrong?* I thought about all the things I loved as a kid, and yet I was doing none of them. I felt trapped by the belief that it was too late to change. This inauthentic life took a toll on my physical and mental health.

I was diagnosed with chronic fatigue syndrome (CFS) and then depression. I felt completely helpless and housebound. At this point, I was aware that I had a choice – either succumb to the depression and in a way give up on a fulfilling life, or find a solution to recover and thrive.

After seeing countless doctors for advice, I finally found a wonderful doctor who reminded me of Clive James sitting in his old chair. He was the first to diagnose my CFS and asked me to bring in a sample of everything I ate over a week. He held a sample to my cheek and tried to push my extended arm down with his other hand. When touching foods I was sensitive or weak to, my arm collapsed from his pressure. I had him try Vegemite countless times, but tragically to no avail. This was the beginning of my diet change. I removed gluten, dairy, preservatives and meat from my diet and started a full plant-based diet. This played a big role in restoring my health, and I'm glad I persisted in searching for the right doctor for me. I felt like a bit of a broken record in countless waiting rooms, but my persistence paid off.

Although I was not well enough to work back in IT, I was able to work in a local timber yard, and I joined a local triathlon group. This physical activity, from both my work and exercise, helped me gain self-respect and therefore started to restore my health and wellbeing. I no longer craved the boozy nights out until the early hours of the morning. Instead, I craved going to bed early and getting up early, heading into St Kilda to race, while others were on their way home from a big night out.

In 2002, I was back in IT, but still not 100 percent mentally. I had the opportunity to work in Germany and took the plunge. Although it was a great experience, I knew deep down I was not happy. In 2005, I was ready for a change and headed west to Perth for an IT job. Some new friends talked me into doing the Western Australian Ironman. As part of my training, I did yoga and met a lady named Marina, whose name means 'of the sea'. I was content in Western Australia and started dabbling in the things I loved as a kid, such as watching nature docos and my art.

Little did I know, however, how my life was about to dramatically change.

In 2006, I boarded my first Sea Shepherd vessel, the *Farley Mowat*, in Melbourne. As part of the tour, I was shown a video where I saw whales being killed and heard the words of Sea Shepherd founder, Captain Paul Watson. With tears in my eyes, a lump in my throat and a fire in my belly, his words and passion hit home.

To me, nature has and always will be the greatest and most spectacular show on earth. However, as I learnt through Captain Watson, not only is nature amazing, but our very survival depends on it. Put so effectively with Watson's spaceship earth analogy, the trees, bees, wolves, whales, sharks down to plankton, regulate our climate, and they provide us with the food we eat and the air we breathe. They maintain the life support systems of spaceship earth. Humans are just the passengers. The problem is that we are rapidly killing off the crew, instead of protecting it.

At the end of the day, we can have all the cures in the world for people, but it will be all for nothing if we do not protect the very life support systems that make it possible for us to exist. In simple terms, putting nature first, is putting humanity first. I knew this instinctively as a boy, yet I lost it temporarily along the way.

Two pivotal moments helped me find myself again.

In 2006, on a road trip from Perth to Melbourne, Marina and I stopped at the Bunda cliffs, which stretch 100 kilometres long and soar up vertically to 100 metres. Looking over the side at the turquoise ocean below, we saw southern right whales, a mother and her baby. Like a rumble of thunder before a storm hits, we knew these whales were a sign of changes to come.

The second pivotal moment was triggered by the passing of Steve Irwin. I reflected on his life and thought that with people like him around, nature stood a chance. I also thought that although he died young at 44, he lived a full and passionate life. What is the point in living to be 100 in a life without passion and meaning? It was time to change.

So, I decided to volunteer at Australia Zoo, to test the waters, and although picking up 'roo poo' wasn't exactly what

I wanted to do, it was nice to be outside and not doing IT. When I arrived back in Fremantle, I actually met Captain Watson, who was trying to get a hold of Terri Irwin to seek permission to name one of Sea Shepherd's vessels, the *Steve Irwin*. The contacts I had made at Australia Zoo facilitated the permission from Terri to make this a reality.

When Operation Migaloo, our 07/08 Antarctic whale defence campaign, was launched, I flew to Melbourne, taking ten days off work to assist in getting the ship ready. I watched it officially christened and named the *Steve Irwin* by Terri, and then I painfully watched the crew sail away without me on board. However, during the third leg of that campaign, I got my chance to join the crew. I felt so privileged to see one of the most beautiful places on the planet – Antarctica, a place that should be just left alone.

We arrived in the searching area, in the middle of an ancient world of ice, where mother nature is front and centre. Before me were icebergs the size of cities, penguin colonies and family groups of orcas storming through like the wolves of the sea. Everywhere we looked we saw whales – minke, fin, blue and humpback whales. However, every hour that passed that we were not on the Japanese whale poachers, whales were being killed, so we continued relentlessly on our search.

One day, I was standing at the radar screen on the bridge of the mighty *Steve Irwin* and every ounce of my being told me that we were heading away from the whale poaching fleet. I had studied the weather and ice charts and put myself in the shoes of the poachers. Somehow, I managed to convince Captain Watson to change course to where I thought the whalers were. I was running on adrenalin and following my gut. What if I was wrong? Hundreds of whales would die, and

I'd feel like I had blood on my hands. Added to that pressure was the thought of failing all the good people on board and on the ground globally, who got us to this place at this time.

We carefully picked our way through the ice, navigating through the fog, and within hours we had harpoon kill ships on the radar acting as decoys, trying to take us away from our position. I once again told Captain Watson where I believed the factory ship to be, and our chase continued.

We soon had a much larger target on the radar, and afters hours of hot pursuit (and almost losing one engine), we could finally see the formidable structure of the 8000-tonne whale slaughterhouse, *Nisshin Maru.*

As dawn broke, we closed in on the *Nisshin Maru's* slipway. With the crew elated, a then second mate, Peter Hammarstedt, turned to me and asked if I would do Sea Shepherd and the whales the honour of hoisting the black Sea Shepherd's Jolly Roger flag. With close quarters, armed Japanese coast guards operating in Australian waters threw flash bang concussion grenades onto our ship to intimidate us. A few grenades exploded near me. Fortunately, they are designed to disorientate, not injure – although I didn't know that at the time.

Regardless, we had our prize – the factory ship. By being there and blocking their operations, the harpoon ships couldn't transfer their dead whales, meaning they could not kill live ones. With that, whaling was ended for that Antarctic summer, and 500 whales were spared. I can still remember the text I got from my proud Mum and Dad: '500 whales coming up the coast this year because you acted.'

On route back to Melbourne from the whales' Antarctic feeding grounds, I presented Captain Watson with ideas on how we could grow Sea Shepherd in Australia, to which he presented me with the offer of a volunteer role as Australian Director. With that, my baptism of fire was well and truly realised.

My whole life changed the day I stepped foot on board that black ship in Melbourne in 2006. Had I not followed my heart, I may still be stuck in a work environment that literally made me sick. To be clear, I have nothing against IT, but my heart and my calling were elsewhere.

In life, we all have choices. I chose to not stay in depression, to fight for the life I knew was possible. I left IT and followed my heart to nature and the ocean. Had I not, I would never have been to the extraordinary places I have been, nor met the extraordinary people I have met. I have played key roles in campaigns that range from defending the world's biggest humpback whale nursery off the Kimberley coast, to stopping the Western Australia shark cull, and ending whaling in the Southern Ocean, to safeguarding one of the world's most critical southern right whale nurseries.

With each campaign, the flow of energy creates waves of change in the defence of nature, galvanising more and more people together. With each campaign, my mind, body and soul are nourished. Throughout it all, I have felt privileged to serve the natural world, while humbly and proudly working with countless courageous and selfless 'shepherds of the sea' and First Nations people in Arnhem Land, the Kimberley, and the Bight. What a privilege it has been to learn more about what it means to be truly connected to country. Our First Australians have the knowledge and wisdom to lead us out of this ecological mess. We only need to ask them and listen, for they are ready.

It's been hard at times away from my kids, yet in years to come, when they ask me what I did to help Mother Earth, I can hold my head up high. From when I was a young boy, I knew with every ounce of my fibre what the purpose of my life was – to save life, to save the earth, to make a stand and say enough is enough. And to fight for nature like our lives depended on it, because they do. Since living in alignment with my true nature, my life has been rich and rewarding beyond my imagination.

It's never too late. Follow your heart, live compassionately, and take care of our spaceship. Take a leap of faith, take a step on board, for you never know where your journey may lead you. You may just change yourself, and you may just change the world.

Chapter 28

Chapter 29
The Flying Nun

Sister Anne Maree Jensen

Rising to my calling as a flying nun.

'I became intimately involved in the land and was taught an entirely new spirituality – a new energy, connection, and communal resonance.'

My story began in Toowoomba, where I grew up in a traditional Catholic household, attending weekly Mass, praying the rosary daily, and attending Catholic schools where my faith was nurtured and nourished by the nuns. In 1974, after extensive discernment, I met the challenge to enter Religious Life. I joined the Queensland Presentation Sisters and became a primary school teacher which, I presumed, would be my role for the rest of my life!

For ten years, I taught children in Brisbane, in the country towns of Emerald and Longreach, and finally at the beach at Maroochydore. In 1988, when I was considering other ministries, Father Terry Loth, the Aerial Ministry Priest based in Longreach, approached me to see if I would be interested in continuing the work of the aerial ministry. He explained the role as 'meeting people on a one-to-one basis, preparing the children for the sacraments, and being there for the women'.

I indicated I was interested, and he replied, 'I'm really looking for someone to pilot the plane.'

I thought to myself: *Me? Fly? Could I? I have a car licence and a bus licence. Yes, I am sure I can fly.*

I arrived at Maroochydore Aviation School and found myself among enthusiastic 17-year-old fellows. However, fear dominated me initially. I struggled immensely to learn to fly. And then new questions arose, such as: *Is it appropriate for me, a woman dedicated to God, to fly a plane to isolated places where I might provide ministry for people in remote areas?* It took courage to step beyond that comfortable teacher's role, and I have absolutely no regrets.

When the chief flying instructor ventured up with me in flight, his reassurance encouraged me to persevere. Finally, in 1989, I was granted a license to fly. Then, I was determined that fear would not overwhelm me.

I took to the skies in a single-engine Cessna and, with my aerial maps in hand, I navigated my way to Longreach, which became my home base for the next 12 years. My role was to minister to the spiritual and human needs of the families of the outback, irrespective of their religion.

I spent a year familiarising myself with the plane, learning to navigate over vast terrain and remote distances south and west of Longreach. In this vast area of Queensland, people live in small towns and on pastoral properties, managing livestock. The area covered was 250,000 square kilometres – larger than the state of Victoria. The United Kingdom has a slightly smaller area, and it had a population of 57 million. The population of the area I covered was approximately 1500 people.

Although I was assured that I would never be 'lost', there were many times when I flew to a waterhole with the sun shining on it, thinking it was the roof of a homestead. With a lack of landmarks for guidance, I needed to adapt to the vastness and remoteness of the land. Perseverance, determination, and the generous people of the land motivated and encouraged me to embrace ministry.

Struggles and challenges included maintaining familiarity with the operation of a single-engine four-seater Cessna 172 aircraft and navigating over the vastness of the land. On a couple of occasions, the possibility of finding my way through dust storms and flying around thunderstorms created mental anguish.

My personal struggles included being on the move continually and sleeping in a different bed each night. During that time, I had no set diet or exercise program. The working days were long, with little time for myself.

Understanding the needs of people living in remote areas raised questions regarding my suitability for the ministry. The challenge, from my perspective, was to understand what it was like to live in a remote area. Death was a confronting challenge, with multiple forms of loss and grief in the families' lives. The pain and anguish of officiating at a funeral of an 18-month-old child who died in a posthole on the property remains with me. However, it was the people's courage, resilience, and tenacity to overcome their challenges that inspired me to overcome mine.

Moreover, I was well supported. There were competent 'bush mechanics' who skilfully cared for vehicles and, at times, my aircraft. Thankfully, in Longreach, a reliable aircraft mechanic was also available when needed.

With significant support from my family, the Leadership Team and Sisters of my Religious Congregation, the people in the Dioceses of Rockhampton and Toowoomba, and many priests who accompanied me through the years, I never felt alone.

On the dashboard of my plane, I had the words of a favourite hymn of mine: 'I will be your God who flies with you'. So, with God by my side, I was never alone.

During the 12 years in the outback, I was gifted with the experience of expanses of sparse land and the remoteness of communities. Having heard, shared, and reflected on the multi-faceted lives of the people, I have been profoundly moved by their qualities of resilience, courage, and compassion. The experiences we exchanged nourished our friendships. I was particularly drawn to the courage and resilience of the women.

Although my role was described as a 'Ministry of Presence',

I learnt that this was not a one-way presence. There was a mutuality whereby I learnt values of flexibility, generosity, spirituality, hospitality, and toughness in the event of nature's challenges of drought and flood. The bonds of kinship were nourished by sharing the same challenges and struggles, the same joys and delights, and communicating in the language of kindness and generosity. This sacred experience added greater depth and quality to my spiritual life. They have instilled a lasting memory of goodness that continues to inspire me long after my time in the outback.

As I reflect on that time, I cherish the honour and privilege that were generously extended to me. Now, I offer a prayer of gratitude for the beauty of the land and its people, the gift of the journey, and the joy of companionship. This time with remote rural families contributed profoundly to my personal development and the unfolding direction of my life's pathway. The lessons that made a significant difference to me then, continue to profoundly influence me today.

I learnt a most valuable lesson when first meeting the people of outback Queensland. There was an unspoken invitation to 'come and experience' our lifestyle, our spirituality. I learnt that the spirituality of the bush is tied irrevocably to the land and its people. Due to the nature of the land – that is, its isolation and harshness – the people who live and breathe in daily isolation are largely self-sufficient yet aware of their dependency needs.

Through their self-reliance, they have developed outstanding adaptability. For example, creatively, they fix machines that break down. When items are missing from the pantry, they improvise, or do without. They confront bull dust, potholes, and corrugation, challenging their safety as they travel remote routes. The Flying Doctor visited once a month, but their services might not be accessed when unexpected illness occurred. Many women were adept at diagnosing symptoms and consulting with doctors by phone.

Another valuable lesson I learnt was to be deeply focused when a woman shared her struggles and concerns. All that was required of me was to offer an attentive ear and a compassionate heart. On several occasions, I was the only female the woman had seen in the previous month. Other visitors were usually male – the truck driver, mailman, refueller, stock agents and bosses.

Emotional challenges confronted me. These arose during my regular visits to a middle-aged woman who knew she was dying. She took comfort and support as I listened to her expression of anguish. As her own body deteriorated, she was conscious of the suffering of her family as they struggled with the reality of her imminent death. My presence with her provided a compassionate listener to whom she could express the depth of her fears at leaving her loved ones. I have sat with a young wife whose husband had been killed recently in a plane crash while mustering on their property. I have been in a home when the phone rang and a child who was away at boarding school expressed loneliness at being far away from home and family.

In listening with the heart, I learnt not to internalise multiple burdens and to avoid absorbing human pain. Reflecting on my pastoral skills, I learnt that my own resilience increased. This enabled me to be attentive to concerns and worries, and then to surrender the outcome to a loving, tender and gracious God. Each night in prayer, I expressed gratitude for having shared the trust of people, who communicated their precious and sacred stories with me. My prayer each morning was: *Help me Gracious God to be present to whoever needs me this day.*

Having participated in the lives of the people of the outback and being influenced by their resourcefulness, my own life underwent profound change. Currently, I am a Pastoral Care Worker in a Residential Aged Care Facility. My care and compassion for the families of the outback have enabled me to open my heart and spirit to the residents in aged care. I have new insights into the struggles of battlers, stronger dedication, and a fuller passion, appreciation and understanding of human nature.

Women were the backbone that kept their rural places viable. The women were the homemakers, educators, nurses, secretaries, bookkeepers, financial managers, electricians and gardeners. Many of the women came from somewhere else to the outback as governesses, teachers, or nurses. They adapted to the rigors of heat, flies, dust, wind, and insects, and adjusted to the lack of mod cons. However, the men have generally always lived in the outback. They are more predictable. In marrying rural men, women made a lifetime commitment to their marriage, to family life, to their community, to their lifestyle, and to the land. They truly are the unsung heroes.

My new comfort zone emerged when I realised that I was a sounding board and that I offered friendship and support. I became intimately involved in people's lives, from birth to death and all of life in between. I became intimately involved in the land and was taught an entirely new spirituality – a new energy, connection and communal resonance.

In the outback, questions surfaced. How did isolated people who rarely saw a priest nurture and sustain their faith? In inviting me to 'come and see', they taught me the value of community and helping neighbours, even if this meant a three-hour round trip. They taught me the beauty of nature, of a night sky and a setting sun.

I saw and witnessed Dorothea McKellar's description:

> *I love a sunburnt country,*
> *A land of sweeping plains,*
> *Of ragged mountain ranges,*
> *Of droughts and flooding rains.*
> *I love her far horizons,*
> *I love her jewel-sea,*
> *Her beauty and her terror –*
> *The wide brown land for me!*

Dorothea McKellar's 1906 poem *My Country*

In communicating with people who are struggling, I would advise them to validate and acknowledge their experienced pain and struggles, believing that this too would pass.

For people who are struggling, I would encourage them to become aware of the negative thought patterns that might be dragging them down and to look for ways of reframing their struggle to move them to consider alternative values to give meaning and purpose to their life. I would encourage them to look for little glimpses that show a light at the end of the tunnel and to seek help when problems seem insurmountable. Finally, I would say to them: *be grateful, find your passion – and own and live your dream.*

Chapter 29

Chapter 30

Keeping the Snake Outside

Natalie Stockdale

Rising from droughts, divorce and disease.

*'If we work on our character,
our character will work for us.'*

As a young married couple, we lived in a cottage on a sheep and cattle station not far from Longreach in outback Queensland. I was a teacher at the 'School of the Air', and my husband was a station overseer. Although we were content, we both sought more excitement, adventure and challenge.

In the early 90s, the wool market collapsed, and drought was beginning to grip the region. Land prices plummeted, and sheep were being given away by the truckloads. We therefore saw this as an opportunity to buy our own property. Enter ... Tocal Station – 60,000 acres of what was then hungry, desolate country with rundown infrastructure and 100 kilometres west of Longreach, along a dry-weather-only road.

With unbridled optimism, we embraced our new life as graziers. We thought: *it's gotta rain soon* and *the wool prices will pick up.*

How naive we were.

Droughts have a slow, insidious effect – constantly worrying about the starving animals and growing debt, they wear you down. I felt guilty each time I flushed the loo, knowing that the house dam was shrinking with each press of the button. Twice a day, I'd do a 'water run' to either save sheep who were bogged in the drying water holes, or to end the suffering of the sheep who couldn't stand up or had their eyes stolen by the crows. I'd point a gun to their head and whisper, 'I'm sorry' as I shot each one. I'd then get back in the Toyota to drive to the next dam and repeat it all again.

One day, while checking the last dam, I came across two wethers (castrated male sheep) who were firmly bogged in the thick black silt. *Here we go again*, I thought. I took off my shorts and waded in, mud sucking my legs with each heavy step. The crows had beaten me to the first sheep. I pulled him out and carried him to the bank. As he lay silently in blindness, I pointed the rifle to his head and, as always, pulled the trigger. Then I dragged him to the pile of rotting corpses beside the dam, sorry for the lack of dignity bestowed to his little body, sorry for his suffering, sorry for 'everything'.

The second sheep had also lost his eyes but, thankfully, was no longer suffering. This sheep, however, presented another problem. He was a few metres in from the edge. In some dams, the silt was up to two metres deep.

I spotted an old piece of corrugated tin on the bank of the dam and dragged it onto the silt. It would be my bridge between the bank and the dead sheep. I made tentative, baby steps to the end of the tin, crouched down and reached out as far as I could. I gripped the wool in my hands, then after the count of three, I heaved with all my strength.

Suddenly, the tin slipped backwards and catapulted me headfirst over the dead sheep, into the cesspool of slime, wool, rotting flesh and bones. I scuttled out of the water, spitting and blowing the muck from my mouth and nose. Filthy, wet and smelly, I sat next to the pile of dead sheep and contemplated. *Surely, it can't get any worse than this?*

The windmill creaked with a macabre snigger.

It didn't rain on Tocal for another two years.

In desperation, we decided to shoot 2000 starving sheep to end their suffering. We set up portable steel enclosures on a claypan about ten kilometres away from the homestead and slowly walked the mob into what became the killing yards. While I walked beside them on my horse, my husband crawled the ute behind the tail of the mob, picking up the weakest ones who collapsed on their way. Once they were all enclosed, my husband began the long, heart-breaking task of shooting each one. The bang of the bullets followed my horse and I all the way home and marked one of our saddest days.

Most of my 20s and 30s were in the bush where my 'resilience muscle' worked hard and grew. As well as the droughts, I battled with brown snakes (once in the middle of the night in my nightie, while pregnant), had medical emergencies while the roads were wet and impassable, and there were plenty of flood dramas when the big rains finally came. Sometimes, when my husband was away working on other stations, I wouldn't see another human for weeks. After a big rain, we were cut off from town for up to six weeks.

Life wasn't easy, but I developed a set of resilience tools that served me well for such challenges. I wasn't aware at the time how my healthy lifestyle habits – diet, sleep, and daily exercise – were creating a strong mind-body foundation to help me cope with the stressors.

I adapted quite well to the absence of human company, by enjoying the company of animals. Our chooks were individually named. Blue Legs, the bantam, would pop up to the veranda and sit on my lap. Basil, our 'poddy' sheep, would join my little menagerie on our sunset walks along the dirt tracks with the kelpies, Jack Russell terriers and, remarkably, Tom the cat. Sometimes I'd carry a handsaw on our sunset walks and cut mulga branches for Basil.

Although geographically isolated, I kept social contact through the phone, HF radio and old-fashioned letters. Social connection with neighbours was particularly important during droughts. One of our neighbours was dear Mrs Rogers, a widow who managed her station alone. We called each other weekly to stay connected and boost our morale.

A friendly phone call can make all the difference to someone who's battling alone. I mostly said 'yes' to invitations, even when they were hundreds of kilometres away, because I'd always return home feeling a little restored.

Self-care was another strategy I used in the bush. I did things that made me feel better, even for a short time. I found creative ways to relax – cooking, painting the house, and creating a 'resilient' garden. Sometimes we'd drive to what remained of our 'permanent' waterhole on the Thomson River and have a picnic with neighbours and friends. We grabbed those little bites of joy and savoured them until next time.

Gratitude was one of my most valuable inner resources. Although I was sometimes overwhelmed by all the death and suffering of the animals, I consciously appreciated the 'gold' in my life – my husband (even though he was often away), our three healthy daughters who came later, my animal friends, my human friends, our house, space, freedom, good health, the wildlife, magnificent sunsets, and the many adventures that were unique to the outback. Even in tough times, there's always something for which to be grateful.

On the odd occasion, my husband and I left little notes to each other that said: 'I love you'; 'I'm so proud of you'; 'Another day closer to rain. We'll get through this'. They were like coaching notes to gently push each other on and help us feel appreciated and positive.

I found Abraham Lincoln's principle of 'this too shall pass' to be greatly comforting. Of course, it would rain again one day. Of course, the grass will grow again. Of course, the (surviving) animals would thrive ... and they did.

Around 2006, my husband had enough of grazing, so we sold our property and opened ourselves to a new adventure. It was one of those rare and exciting gaps of time when we had a blank canvas to create a completely new life in which we could all thrive and try to make the world a little better.

Open to a world of possibilities, we let our hearts lead the way and booked our individual dream holidays. I went to the Bahamas to swim with wild dolphins. Unfortunately, Hurricane Rita struck at the same time, rendering the sea too hazardous for swimming. However, after Rita passed, our group was able to *sail* with dolphins, and there I found my bliss. It was the first time I had ever been on a yacht and the first time I had seen dolphins. I was thrilled by their energy, speed, endurance and playfulness, and when they rolled over slightly to make eye contact, that was it! Stamped – ocean life was for me!

After my husband and I reunited from our respective trips, we decided to find a place on the east Australian coast where we could create a new life that merged our respective new passions. Enter ... the ruggedly beautiful Sapphire Coast of New South Wales.

A friend playfully called our new home 'Happy Valley' because we were all happy in our green, undulating valley with a lake, a river 'beach' and a menagerie of dogs, horses, 'celebrity' pet pigs (from the *Charlotte's Web* movie) and chooks – all happily free-ranging together in a sprawling, picturesque paddock. I bought a French yacht and ran an eco-tourism business – sailing with dolphins and whales. Sharing the magic of joy, awe, gratitude, humility, and the excitement of being on the ocean with marine animals gave me great pleasure.

Chapter 30

I remember one well-travelled gentleman who was celebrating his 60th birthday on a private charter. I stayed up late the night before to make him a surprise, giant chocolate cake. The moment the wind filled the sails and we were off, the cake slipped and splatted onto the floor. After scooping up the remnants onto the platter, it looked like a lump of horse manure. Thankfully, he wasn't there for my fine cuisine! He was there for the whales — and they didn't disappoint. At the end of the day, he said it was the greatest experience of his life: 'better than the pyramids of Egypt!'

Every day, back then, was filled with love, joy and sincere appreciation. Appreciation for the obvious things – our family and new home – but also appreciation for things that came from the contrast of the outback: the 'normal' schools for our daughters, a school bus, bitumen roads, wheelie bins, clean house water (which meant white clothes), listening to heavy rain without worrying about animals being washed away, and only a 20-minute drive to town in any weather. Hard times teach us gratitude for the good times. Indeed, these were good, though short-lived times.

While my 'resilience muscle' served me well in previous challenges, I was ill-prepared for what was about to happen.

At the start of 2009, my husband ended our marriage and 're-partnered' with another woman. It felt like a death. Not only the death of our marriage, our family unit, our home and dreams. It was the death of an age of innocence – for my girls and me. Gone was our 'Happy Valley'. Gone was that deep sense of trust that 'all will be well'.

In the aftermath of our separation, I moved into a rented house near the girls' school, closed my business, sold our yacht and property. I worked voluntarily for an animal protection organisation, while exploring new ways to support myself and my girls. By this stage, I had acquired (remotely) a post-graduate degree in Animal Welfare and was soon offered a highly sought-after job as a Humane Educator in Melbourne. This, I thought, was my best opportunity to move on, provide for my girls, model a work ethic for my girls and contribute to a kinder world. However, with the girls' understandable aversion to cities, they chose to stay with their father in their familiar surrounds. So, I promised it would be temporary, and that one day, we'd be together again, somehow.

Broken-hearted, I drove away, watching my girls huddling and crying together. It is a reflection that haunts me to this day.

I loathed living in the city. I pined for my girls, my home, animals and friends, yet I pushed through because I lacked the skills at that stage to manage the trauma and make a better decision. Stress, I learnt years later, impedes various cognitive functions, including decision-making.

Most of the resilience tools that served me well in the bush were no longer accessible. I no longer had my family, animals, nature, or social support. Ironically, in a city with millions of people, I was never lonelier.

Moreover, because I was disconnected from everything I loved, I was living *inauthentically*. My outer world (yang) was completely disjointed from my inner world (yin). This incongruence heightened my stress.

It was the first (and only) time in my life that I struggled to practise gratitude. Instead, I harboured negative emotions – blame, resentment, anger, deep sadness, and an ocean of guilt about the girls. I didn't know then that by holding on to negative emotions, we exhaust our biological stress response, evaporate our energy reserves, collapse our innate healing systems, and render ourselves vulnerable to disease.

Decades of scientific research by the HeartMath Institute has proven that ongoing worry and negative projections take a toll on our mental and emotional state, and eventually our physical health. My life, therefore, became a recipe for disease.

Unsurprisingly, 18 months after our marriage ended, I was staring at an x-ray on a wall with an oncologist.

'There it is,' she said. 'Solid in the centre. Blurry on the outside. Classic cancer.'

Without a word of reassurance, I thought I was going to die. I wasn't particularly afraid of dying, as I'd be in peace. My greatest fear was causing further distress to my girls and elderly parents. Breaking the news to them was awful. Being filthy, wet and smelly back on that dam bank with a pile of dead sheep was much easier.

I don't know how I would have coped through this time without my mother, who accompanied me to every hospital appointment and treatment. On one occasion, my hospital appointment clashed with her own medical appointment, which she insisted she would cancel to be with me. 'Don't be silly,' I said. 'Go to *your* appointment. I'll be fine alone.'

Afterall, I knew aloneness well.

The moment I stepped through the hospital doors, however, my bravado evaporated, and I missed my mum. Unbeknown to me, Mum's companionship and banter had buffered me from the sadness, sickness and clinical coldness inherent in hospitals. From then on, I was more appreciative of Mum's support and agreed that she accompany me every time.

One afternoon, while in hospital recovering from a nine-hour mastectomy and complex breast reconstruction surgery,

I read a poem that was written and kindly sent to me by primatologist and conservationist, Dr Jane Goodall, who I had met through my animal welfare work:

'Requiem of the Breast'

Once you were not.
Now you are not again.
I was without. I am without once more.
But such a tiny loss because
I have my arms and legs, my hands
And feet. I have my lungs and heart,
My liver and my spleen. And oh! I have
My eyes and nose, my mouth and ears
And teeth. I have my smile. I have
My soul, my spirit self, my inner Me.
Poor breast. I sorrow at the ease with which
I can dispense with thee.

As every woman who's had a mastectomy knows, *dispensing with thee* is not so easy. Nonetheless, Jane was right. It could have been worse.

A couple of nurses bowled into my ward with the sensitivity of jackhammers.

'More bloods!' announced one of them.

Behind a fragile veil of courage, I protested, 'But I've already given blood *twice* today. Surely that's enough!'

'No. Our instructions are to get more.'

'My arm is sore and swollen. Please, I *really* don't want to give any more.'

'Your bloods have gone missing! We must get more,' they demanded.

I feebly surrendered my arm as they pierced a needle into my veins again … and again and couldn't extract any more blood, not a drop. The other nurse tried again and again, with the same result.

When they eventually left the room, I burst into tears. Was I crying for my arm? Was I crying for my breast, my aching body, my cancer? Was I crying because I felt violated by the 'vampires', or betrayed by my husband? Was I missing my daughters? Was I grieving for the family, animals, home, and the dreams I had lost?

It wasn't a 'falling off your bike' cry, or a 'sad film' cry. It was a long-overdue, heavy, inconsolable release for all the above.

My girls, who were then living near Melbourne with their father, came to visit me in hospital a day or two later. While it was hard for them to see me 'tubed up' and battered, it was equally hard for me to see their distress. My middle daughter, Eliza, aged 12 at the time, intuitively sat on the floor at the foot of my bed, facing away from me, and began playing her flute. I can't remember what she played, but she switched the focus away from my condition, and through her music, she filled the room with exactly what we needed – love.

I liken my cancer survival to having a snake removed from my house. Thanks to the brilliant surgeons, the snake's outside, but if I didn't figure out how it entered in the first place, it could slip back in.

Before my cancer, my body was healthy. I had never smoked a cigarette in my life. I ate well, exercised every day, breastfed each of my babies until they were 15 months and had no history of breast cancer in my family. So why did I get it? My oncologists explained that it was 'random', 'just bad luck, like being struck by lightning'. I knew, however, that in my case, there was more to the story.

After a full recovery and voluntary work in Africa (to help an animal protection campaign, *and* take my mind off myself), I began work as CEO for the Jane Goodall Institute Australia, a global organisation that promotes the protection of Great Apes and compassion to all life. The job was meaningful and an honour, yet I continued to wonder why I became so sick and what lessons my body was teaching me.

This curiosity grew into a passion for wellness and personal development. Years later, I resigned from my job and dived into the study of Mind Body Medicine therapies. From this education, I realised that my cancer was enabled by the way I handled my stress, or *mishandled* it. Resilience is an antidote to stress, and my resilience resources were insufficient.

It's important here to distinguish between blaming myself for my illness (which would cultivate more negative, unhealthy emotions) and simply observing that had I understood the mind-body connection and had effective resilience resources, I would have been less stressed, able to make better decisions, my immune system would have been stronger, and I would have been less likely to open the door to cancer. However, I managed the stress the best way I could with the resources I had at the time.

To keep that snake outside my house, I realised (eventually) that I needed to learn and adopt healthy *new* ways to reduce stress. I needed a comprehensive and robust bank of resilience tools.

Tools like the 'Stockdale Paradox'. This has also been mentioned in Lindy Chamberlain-Creighton's story, and I'd like to elaborate on it a little more here.

The Stockdale Paradox was named after James Stockdale, a United States Navy Vice Admiral and fighter pilot, who was imprisoned at the notorious 'Hanoi Hilton' during the Vietnam War. (Our ancestral link – unknown, possible, hopeful!)

In 1965, Stockdale was shot down over Vietnam. As he descended by parachute onto enemy ground, fully aware that he'd be captured, he knew that he would need to apply his wisdom to survive his new world. He also knew it would be a turning point in his life. Stockdale was *prepared for pain*.

And pain he endured in mighty doses. Over seven years, Stockdale was chained, malnourished, tortured and solitarily confined, without any rights or release date. Extraordinarily, he adapted positively to these conditions. While believing that he'd be free one day, he accepted the reality of being in prison for the long-term. He accepted his fate and decided he would do everything he could to protect his survival and that of his fellow prisoners. To that end, he merged optimism with realism.

Stockdale was released in 1973 and awarded the Medal of Honour for his bravery. In a subsequent interview about his resilience, Stockdale said, 'You must never confuse faith that you will prevail in the end – which you can never afford to lose – with the discipline to confront the most brutal facts of your current reality, whatever they might be.'[i]

According to Stockdale, the prisoners who believed that their freedom was just around the corner and didn't face the reality of their situation were grief-stricken when their freedom didn't come.

---

i   J Collins, *Good to Great: Why Some Companies Make the Leap ... and Others Don't*, Random House Business Books, London, 2001.

The optimists, said Stockdale, were the ones who died. They didn't die from the torture or hardship. 'They died of a broken heart.'[ii]

Indeed, optimism alone, is not enough.

Forever grateful for Stockdale's legacy, I now use the Stockdale Paradox as my principal tool to overcome any challenging situation. Regardless of the matter, I know that I'll be ok – which is my optimism. At the same time, I face the reality and ask myself what other tools I need to help me. It could, for example, be practical actions to rectify the problem. Once I take those actions, I immediately feel relief that progress is underway.

Sometimes, in distressing circumstances, we may need more than practical actions to feel better. We may need to transform our negative, depleting emotions to positive, restorative emotions to maintain a healthy mind and body. On these occasions, I make a mental list of other tools to engage.

If I feel stress, I practise a mindfulness technique that harmonises my brain with my heart to restore mind-body balance. I also remind myself that the stress will pass – the principle of temporariness. I sometimes chat with friends or family (social support), dip into the ocean (nature therapy), or go for a walk (exercise), usually with whatever music lifts me.

I also ask myself what character virtues would help me. Virtues are the elements of our character, our powerful inner resources, and they can be our greatest allies during hard times. If we work on our character, our character will work for us.

To heal from my marriage break-up, I needed the virtue of forgiveness. I needed to forgive my ex-husband, and also

---

ii ibid.

myself for the mistakes I made after our separation. I was able to forgive only when I understood that everyone is imperfect. Our actions stem from a web of interdependent, convoluted influences, deriving from multiple generations. We're all doing our best to 'observe, learn, grow and love' in our individual journeys. Therefore, we don't need to take our own mistakes, or the actions of others, so personally.

Forgiveness doesn't mean endorsing the actions that caused our pain. It means choosing to interpret them in a less personal way. By choosing forgiveness, we transform toxic emotions (resentment etc.) to healthier emotions (joy, appreciation, indifference etc.). Forgiveness enables us to detach, heal and be free.

Similar to forgiveness is detachment – an often misunderstood and under-valued ally in difficult times. Detachment doesn't mean not caring. It means stepping back and looking at the matter with objectivity and poise. With detachment, we can sometimes avoid chaos and drama. By remembering that each of us are on our own journeys, we can choose to not let other people's choices harm us. Detachment can be useful when we're triggered by something done or said to us.

I recall using detachment in a swimwear shop one day, not long after one of my cancer surgeries, which left a prominent scar across my belly from hip to hip. When I explained to the sales assistant that I'd like high-cut bikini pants to cover my scar, she quipped, 'Breast cancer these days is like catching a cold. You get a little sniffle, then get over it.'

Although I was instantly offended – on behalf of the many people who have died or suffered, directly or indirectly, from the disease – I reminded myself that she was just doing her best with her level of experience, then I let it go. Instead of letting her words upset me, I detached. With detachment, we experience emotions, but we don't let them control us. Mind you, I'm quite sure I *didn't* buy her bikinis!

Acceptance is another virtue that I learnt to practise. When we accept what has happened, like James Stockdale did while in prison, we ease the torment and allow ourselves to find peace. Acceptance is being open to 'what is' rather than wishing for something different. When we accept the reality of situations, we open ourselves to new opportunities, which can sometimes be exciting. If we address what we can and accept what we can't, it's easier to find peace.

Confidence is a virtue that I needed to rebuild. Being offloaded after a 23-year relationship, I subconsciously believed that I wasn't good enough. I tried to convince myself otherwise, but that stubborn, inner critic thought she knew better. After cancer came along and I subsequently lost a breast and a job, that inner critic grew louder and stronger. In my mind, I was … obsolete.

I didn't understand then that we can *choose* how to interpret events. By being the gatekeeper of our mind, we can prevent unhealthy thoughts and emotions, such as unworthiness, from sabotaging us.

The importance of mastering our thoughts and emotions is conveyed in a popular Cherokee parable:

A long time ago sat a boy and his grandfather. The boy was tormented by conflicting thoughts, which he said were two wolves fighting in his head. One wolf had angry, bitter, resentful, greedy, vengeful thoughts. The second wolf had calm, peaceful, kind, forgiving, loving thoughts.

He asked, 'Which wolf will win?'

His grandfather answered, 'The one you feed.'

Regardless of how dire our situation may be, our thoughts can worsen our suffering, or they can help us recover. I'm now acutely aware of my thoughts and, if they're not serving me well, I delete them and replace them with healthier thoughts. I feed the *good* wolf.

I also learnt to *guard* my confidence by being more discerning about the company I keep. Sometimes, this has meant letting go of people. It took me many years and 'teachers' to not confuse tolerance, kindness and understanding with self-sacrifice.

Resilient people are often at risk of unhealthy relationships and harsh situations because we *can* tolerate pain. We choose to 'put up' with unkind behaviour because we believe 'they're doing their best', or 'I'll be right'. This can be remedied, however, through being kinder to ourselves and raising the bar of kindness we expect from others.

I wish I knew this back in 1999 around the time of the birth of my third daughter, Zara, at the Longreach Hospital. Days later, we returned home to our new station on the Barcoo River, Honan Downs. There, my husband and I decided that 'I'll be right' if he goes away to work on another station (220 kilometres away) for a week or two, while I take care of ours. That meant looking after two little girls, Sophie and Eliza, newborn Zara, about 5000 sheep, stockhorses, five kelpies, a bunch of Jack Russell terriers, chooks, a large garden, an orchard and ... oh ... heal from childbirth at the same time.

Our rationale was something like ... if peasant women in Asia can work in crops, have a baby then keep working ... 'I'll be right'.

My mother kindly helped me at the start, then, after insisting that 'I'll be right', it was up to me. Three weeks after Zara's birth, she rolled for the first time in her life and fell off her changing table, hitting her head on a rocking horse on her way down. I called a nurse from the Isisford medical clinic, who immediately drove out to check Zara. There was cause for concern, and she needed to go to hospital urgently. I packed the three little girls in the Toyota and rushed 120 kilometres to town.

On the way, a tyre was punctured. A neighbour kindly came to our rescue, changed the tyre and took Sophie and Eliza back to his home. All the way to the hospital, I mercilessly scalded myself. *My poor baby. Will she be damaged? What sort of mother leaves her newborn on a change table? Everyone knows that golden rule!*

The setting sun distorted my vision as we finally approached the hospital. We were almost there, then, *woosh*, a train appeared in my rear-vision mirror. We had just crossed a railway line and missed a collision with the train by a second.

Zara and I stayed in hospital that night. Zara was monitored and was thankfully safe and well. When my husband was told what had happened, he chose not to return home, and I wasn't surprised. We conditioned ourselves into believing that I didn't need softness, warmth or kindness. While both Zara and I did 'get over it', the ordeal could have been prevented, had I been kinder to myself by not taking care of a pastoral station days after giving birth. Had I been kinder to myself, I would have expected greater kindness from my husband.

My subconscious sense of self-sacrifice or self-neglect has since been overthrown. When it reappears, as it occasionally does, self-compassion blows it out like a birthday candle.

Chapter 30

The virtue of authenticity has also been a valuable ally. I changed my life to realign my yang with my yin, to live authentically again, in harmony with my core values. For me, that means family, genuine friends, nature, the ocean, animals, sailing, adventure, and meaningful work – helping people to find happiness through my story writing and coaching. It took me 11 years before I could buy another yacht and be on the sea again. In this environment, where I now live, I feel congruent, nourished and grateful. In this environment, I'm not spared, but cushioned from life's ongoing bumps.

The key to rising from hardship is being prepared for it, with internal and external resources that enable us to survive and flourish.

This was reaffirmed to me in 2021 when I sailed with friends from south-east Queensland to the Whitsundays over two weeks. Although we hoped for favourable conditions all the way, we were prepared for tough conditions, which inevitably struck. We had a life raft, torches, life jackets, emergency beacons, rubber plugs and other safety equipment, which we thankfully didn't need.

However, we did need extra fuel to carry us through the strong headwinds, as well as tools to quickly fix the engine when it stopped in the middle of the ocean … twice. We also had a good crew on board, with the skills and character virtues to get us through the challenges calmly and cheerfully.

The parallel between this sailing journey and other life journeys was not missed. While we had no control over the weather or sea conditions, we were prepared for inevitable rough events with internal and external resources that enabled us to survive and thrive.

During that trip, we discovered a rusty link in the anchor chain. A link that could have snapped and set the yacht adrift onto rocks, or a reef while we slept. With bolt-cutting surgery, we cut the link out and repaired the chain. A 20-centimetre chunk of the chain with the rusty link now sits on a shelf in my yacht as a symbol of the preciousness of life. It's not a chain of gloom or fear. It's a chain that reminds me to treasure life, be mindful of its fragility, and to not take anything for granted.

As you sail through your life's storms, summon your resources, discern your learnings, nurture your character, embrace change, and move forward with a sense of faith – that you will prevail.

Afterword
A Tribute to the Human Spirit

Here's to the people who learn, grow and flourish from their hardships, who truly treasure adversity and are curious about what gifts will come from it.

Here's to the people who look ahead towards their next doors of happiness instead of the closed door behind them, who seek experiences to feel alive and nourish their inner longings.

Here's to the people who know that life was not meant to be dull, or stay the same, and that despite what has happened, happiness is in their reach.

Here's to the people who dare to explore, dream, discover, and meet their inner hero in the face of fear and conflict.

Here's to the people who embrace life and never, ever give up.

# Campfire for the Heart

About the Author

Natalie believes that hardships are an inevitable and essential part of life experience that shape our character and enrich our lives. How we handle our hardships is a choice.

Natalie was raised in the country and educated in boarding school and universities in Melbourne. The moment she completed her studies, she took off to the Australian outback, thirsty for adventure and freedom. After teaching in a remote Aboriginal community in the Northern Territory, 'governessing' on an outback sheep station and teaching at 'school of the air', Natalie married and, with her husband, bought a drought-stricken sheep and cattle station near Longreach, Queensland.

There, Natalie's 'resilience muscle' quickly grew through her experiences of long-term solitude, droughts, floods and raising her three daughters in isolation. She learnt the power of gratitude, nature, and relationships with people *and* animals – to restore and maintain wellbeing.

In her late thirties, when Natalie and her husband paused to reassess their lives, she discovered her love of the ocean and whales, bought a yacht and operated a sailing charter business in southern NSW.

Suddenly, in 2009, her world fell apart – losing her marriage, family, home and business. While struggling to manage her trauma, she moved to Melbourne as a Humane Educator and, shortly after, contracted cancer.

After surviving cancer, Natalie eventually woke up to the importance of resilience for managing stress, and for the health of our mind *and* body. She subsequently resigned from her job as CEO of the Jane Goodall Institute Australia, dived into the world of wellness and wrote *Campfire for the Heart* onboard her yacht in Queensland.

On a mission to make happier, resilient people, Natalie is now a Resilience Coach for individuals, organisations and communities.

www.stockdalewellbeing.com

Limit of Liability/Disclaimer of Warranty

The content in *Campfire for the Heart* book is for informational purposes only and is not intended as a substitute for professional advice, diagnosis, or treatment of any health condition. Always consult your qualified health care provider with questions regarding a condition or challenge. Never disregard professional advice or delay seeking help because of content you have found in this book. Reliance on any information provided in the book is solely at the reader's discretion and risk. You and your health care provider must make any final decisions as to what's best for you.

Support Services
Lifeline: 13 11 14
lifeline.org.au

Suicide Call Back Service: 1300 659 467
suicidecallbackservice.org.au

Beyond Blue: 1300 224 636
beyondblue.org.au

MensLine Australia: 1300 789 978
mensline.org.au

For more great titles visit

www.bigskypublishing.com.au